What the bible says to the Black Man

25 PRINCIPLES EVERY BLACK MAN SHOULD KNOW

TREVOR STEWART

William Ford Publishing

Copyright © 2023 by William Ford LLC

All rights reserved.

No portion of this book may be reproduced in any form without written permission from the publisher or author except as permitted by U.S. copyright law.

This publication is designed to provide accurate and authoritative information in regard to the subject matter covered. It is sold with the understanding that neither the author nor the publisher is engaged in rendering legal, investment, accounting, or other professional services. While the publisher and author have used their best efforts in preparing this book, they make no representations or warranties with respect to the accuracy or completeness of the contents of this book and specifically disclaim any implied warranties of merchantability or fitness for a particular purpose. No warranty may be created or extended by sales representatives or written sales materials. The advice and strategies contained herein may not be suitable for your situation. You should consult with a professional when appropriate. Neither the publisher nor the author shall be liable for any loss of profit or any other commercial damages, including but not limited to special, incidental, consequential, personal, or other damages.

All scripture are taken from King James version, Copyright @1982 by Thomas Nelson Inc. Used by permission, All rights reserved.

1st edition 2023

Dedication

I dedicate this book to my father, the late Mr. Walter Stewart. Walter was a remarkable example of what it meant to be a strong black man. His greatness wasn't because he taught his children how to play sports, invest their money, or run a business. He never taught us any of those things, but he taught us principles. Principles to live by. How to treat and respect people. How to take care of your neighbors and family. He taught us how to be dependable and a servant. It is within this book you will find many of those same principles. I hope they bless you as much as they have blessed us.

I dedicate this book to every black man, boy, or child that God has chosen to represent him with melanin in his skin. I pray that this book will help you overcome any challenges or obstacles you may encounter. God has gifted and entrusted you with his image and his likeness. Demonstrate to the world what God looks like to the best of your ability.

I also dedicate this book to my wife, Shondalyn, and to every person who has the assignment of loving a black man. This is for all who accepted the challenge of standing by and standing with black men. When you couldn't articulate it with words, you demonstrated God's love and compassion with your actions. May this book bless you and all the men whom you love. May it express God's clear path for the kings you love so dearly. May God's plan, protection, and provisions be revealed and abide in their lives. That your heart may be rewarded with the compensation and reparations that only God can repay.

Preface

HOW TO USE THIS BOOK

"What the Bible says to the Black man"! Wow! What a title. I've gotten every kind of response you probably can imagine about this book. Well, it's not all about the book but its title. Some were good and uplifting, and others were, well, let's say that most of the words they used you will not find in the Bible. The commentary wasn't surprising at all. What was surprising was where the majority of the comments came from. They came from people first who were not Christians, and second, they were not Black. This intrigued me because, at one point, I almost felt like they were the neighbors who got your mail, opened it, read it, and then had the nerve to question you about your mail. It wasn't addressed to them, and it wasn't speaking to them, yet they wanted to be acknowledged and a response. Of course, I didn't give them one, but every part of me being Black wanted to, but I refrained. Then I remembered it was because of those very types of people that I had to write the book. They had not read the book, chapter, page, or paragraph and felt they could tell you what it contained. I was amazed by all the wrong assumptions but not shocked. I want to thank them for the confirmation that the book is needed now more than ever, but not for those individuals. There are better books that are better suited for them to begin with. Think of it like math. You can't start out doing multiplication and division. You first have to learn how to add and subtract. Before you can do addition and subtraction, you must learn how to count. You can't discuss algebra and geometry with people who can't count. So, I elected not to entertain such foolishness because they are not my target audience for this particular book. This book is for those with a basic concept of God and who know that he exists but needs clarification. It is for those who want to understand how to be both Black and Christian without compromising either. What is the difference? One was a decision made for you by God; the other is a decision you will make on your own. God chose to send you here with darker skin and African heritage. You had no choice in the matter. The other part of being a Christian is totally up to you. You have to be black, but you don't have to be Christian. This book will help you make an informed decision on if Christian living is right for you. This book is going to help you successfully be both. God needs you to demonstrate that it can be done successfully. Yes, despite oppression, slavery, segregation, and racial profiling, you are made in God's image, and he needs you to wear his image well. Not to represent God how the world has portrayed him, but how Christ portrayed him. When the world sees you, they don't see a Christian man because that isn't what they have been programmed to see. This book will interrupt their regularly scheduled programming with new and authentic images of God and of the Black man.

What the Bible says to the Black man is simply a mirror because that is what the Black man is in desperate need of. He needs a mirror so that he can use it to see himself. If any man sees anything other than the image of God when he views himself in the mirror, he is viewing a distorted image. God's intent for man was for him to reflect his nature, his character, and his image on the earth. But we don't see the image of God or his nature because we are not looking in the mirror. Instead of looking in the mirror, we are looking at one another, social media, and television and copying people who are not copying Christ. I can tell a man what is wrong with him, but he will never change until he can see it for himself. It's something about a mirror, and its ability to say nothing, yet it speaks volumes. A mirror will tell you the truth that your friends will not. A mirror can be either your best friend or your worst enemy, but it is neither without a mirror to look into.

I had to write this book to address the cultural differences of being a Black Christian. The truth is that Black Christians interpret Christianity differently from other ethnic groups. Why? Because we interpret life differently from most ethnic groups. We don't have much of a choice. The lens through which we see the world is often very different because what we have been exposed to, witnessed, and experienced is very different. It's not a race on the planet that has experienced what Black people have. This can be frustrating and overwhelming if you ingest too much at once. We have been exposed to a distorted image—a distorted image of God, a distorted image of Christianity, and a distorted image of ourselves. The one place in the world where God said that we could find refuge was in church, and even that has been distorted. I say this confidently because Jesus said," By this shall all men know that ye are my disciples if ye have love one to another." So, it is clear that we have had people running the church who were not disciples of Jesus, nor were they the representatives of God for hundreds of years. Men who have used the Bible as a window to look out of instead of as a mirror to look into. Using it as a window to look out to judge others gave us a distorted view of God, his Son, and ourselves.

This book is written to shed new light on God's actual image and what he intended for mankind. It is intended to change the way Black men view God, his only Son Jesus Christ, and themselves. Using the mirror God has given us, the Bible, we can see all things more clearly.

Several titles reference this book. You may know it as "How to get to know God." You may know it as "25 Scriptures Every Black Man Should Know." You may have heard" it is considered "What the Bible says to the Black man." Regardless of its title, this book was written for one sole purpose. It was written to introduce God to some while explaining Him to others. To illustrate the three aspects of God that every man should know and study. I've simplified a way to read and study the Bible and give readers life application of His Word. I have determined that everything God has done fits into one of three categories; from Genesis to Revelation, it all fits. So, whether you are reading the deep mysteries of the Book of Revelation or one of the divisions of the Book of Psalms, you can gain insight into what God was doing and, in many cases, why he was doing it. All scripture reveals one of three things: God's plan, protection, or provision. We can get to know God and see his actual image through these three precepts.

I wrote this book to uncover the truth of the law of God and the love of God that has been hidden behind the laws of men. Concealed by the judgment of men and misrepresented by the unrighteousness of men. I intended to remove all of the barriers and ignorance that have shackled and handcuffed men from seeing God's plan, protection, and provision. God plans to have an intimate relationship with mankind. It has always been and will always be His plan. He establishes this relationship by revealing His plan, protection, and provisions for your life.

To get the most out of this book, there are a few things you will need to know. The first thing to remember is that you can start reading this book from any chapter you like. The chapters in this book are all related, but you don't have to read them chronologically to understand. Each chapter has its own unique identity and message. So, if you choose to start at chapter nine, you will not be any less informed than if you started at chapter one. Each chapter contains a principle that reveals an aspect of God solely on its own. Everyone is at different points on their journey with God, so feel comfortable starting this book with where you are as an individual. Learn one precept at a time and apply it. However, I suggest reading the intro to each section before diving into a particular chapter. The three preludes are: The Plan of God, the Protection of God, and the Provisions of God. These intros will help you to understand the importance of each section.

Second, this book was written to be a solution to a problem. If this book doesn't address or solve your problem, it didn't meet its goal. We want you to be able to make informed decisions if this book is right for you. I have personally read books that had catchy titles and lofty promises, only to find the book was either too complicated or too vague to help me. I've read the Bible and other books; sometimes, I wished I could ask the author what he meant or elaborate on a particular point. How cool would it be to be able to ask Paul or even Moses a question about their manuscripts? I never want anyone to read anything I have written and feel they must guess what I was trying to say or the meaning. You will find additional information and links to ask questions about this book to fix that. You can email your questions to Trevor@williamford.us. You also can find videos on various topics on our YouTube station, "Getting-to-know-God." You didn't just purchase a book; you bought a resource. Millions of books have been written and read, but the world isn't short on books.

The world is short on resources. Tap into the plan, protection, and provisions of God.

Introduction

I write this book to all men of all ages because, in these pages, we will find the things we need to know and apply to life. At some point, you will have an encounter with something or someone that will remind you that you are Black. That encounter maybe with a person, a lending institution, or even a law enforcement officer. Life will give you many not-so-gentle reminders to remind you that you are Black. You may say you don't need a book to remind you of the fact that you are black. This book isn't to remind you that you are Black because that is not what they want you to forget. Many of the encounters were designed just for the very reason to remind you of your blackness. It's not your being black that they want you to forget. They want you to forget that you are Christian. They aren't challenging your blackness; they are challenging your Christianity. In those moments, you don't lose sight of your blackness; it's your Christianity that is on trial. This is when you will need something to keep you when you can't keep yourself. You will need something that will change and challenge you without breaking you. Something that will comfort, counsel, and correct you regardless of who is present or absent. It will prepare you for the seen and unseen dangers of life and living. You need something to prepare you for the challenges and opportunities that accompany being a man and a black man. Therefore, I write this book to all those who look like me, feel like me, and have experienced what I have experienced. This book is for those who need a road map or a GPS in this journey called life. It is for those who need light in dark places, those who need a word in moments of silence, and those who need a pathway forward.

Why write a book to the Black man and not to all men? You will find that this book is written to all men and about all men. You will just have to find yourself within the pages. You are either the man who is having a black experience or you are the man who is creating the black experience. The fact is that being Black isn't just a color or race; it is an experience. You can have a Black experience without even being Black. It will be those experiences that will enable non-Black people to identify with Black culture. Culture is the greatest reason for this book because there are differences in cultures that must be recognized. African-American culture differs from White American, Asian-American, Hispanic-American, and Native American cultures. Just as Rap music differs from Country music, Heavy Metal, Pop, and Blues are different from Classical music.

When we fail to address cultural nuances, the omission creates a void regarding the life application of God's word. Just as music creates a void when different cultures play it. For example, the same song is played differently depending on the culture. It can be almost unrecognizable depending on the culture it plays in. One culture will emphasize the drum and the rhythm, while another will focus on tempo and pitch. These differences make it necessary to consider culture no matter what subject we are discussing. It is one thing to tell a person what the Bible says, yet it is another to explain it in the content of one's culture. The Bible acknowledges the different traditions and cultures of the people the writers addressed. The writer Paul said in I Corinthians 9:22, "I become all things to all men that I might, by all means, save some." Paul said he would cross cultures and traditional practices to save souls.

Why write a book for black men? To address their unique culture and traditions. To help them overcome the challenges they face for simply being black. To help them understand how to deal with isolation and despising. To help them learn how to live in a land that viewed them as only three-fifths human.

Why write the book to the Black man? What we are called has changed, but how we are treated and viewed has not. We have been referred to as Black, Colored, Negro, Nigger, Afro-American, and now, African-American. The names have changed, but the problem isn't what others call us. The problem is how they view us and the image they see us through. If they view us as a threat, they will treat us as a threat. If they see us as being criminals, they will treat us like criminals. The focus of this book isn't so much on how others see us but on how we see *ourselves*. The names are only symptoms of the disease, and this book focuses on how to cure the disease.

Why write this book to the Black man? I ask you, who is drowning? I believe either you are teaching them how to swim or you are helping them drown. Suppose you believe that the unemployment rate is higher for Black men. In that case, the rate of incarceration is higher among Black men, the number of absent Black fathers is higher than that of other cultures, and the likelihood of being killed in our communities is higher for Black men. It sounds like you agree with the assessment that the Black man is the man who is drowning. If I were a lifeguard, I could throw the rope in two feet of water, three feet, or even ten feet, but that wouldn't save those in twenty and thirty feet. If I throw the rope into the deepest part of the water, I can save those in the deep and shallow water. When I begin to pull the rope in, whether you are in the deep or the shallow, if you grab hold, I can pull all men to shore. Yes, the book is written to the Black man because we are in the deepest water, but this can help save all men, whether in the deep or shallow water. It is the same principle in the emergency room. The patients are triaged and seen according to the severity of their health emergency. From everything that I have observed in life, it is clear which patients are in dire need of treatment.

There are three things that you need from God every day. You need the plan of God, the protection of God, and the provisions of God. This book addresses these things that will make life successful. God's plan, protection, and provision for your life will bring light into darkness and clarity where there was confusion. You should ask God for these basic things every morning before your day begins. The plan of God is His purpose for your life. That is why you are here. The protection of God is so that you can carry out His plan. You can only fulfill the purpose if God protects you from all hurt and harm. The last thing you must have is provision. God has to supply you with the necessary resources to fulfill your purpose. He does that through provisions.

This book will introduce you to three aspects of God.

God the planner, God the protector, and God the provider.

Contents

Chapter

The Plan Of God	1
1. Dominate Rule Reign And Work	7
2. Don't Waste Your Time	17
3. A Changed Mind Equals A Changed Man	23
4. See You At the Finish Line	29
5. Trust the Process	35
6. You Owe Them	41
7. Count up the Cost	47
8. They Become What They See	53
9. What's In The Name	59
The Protection of God	63
10. You Have Help	67
11. Don't Hate The Harvest	73

12.	Don't Use the Wrong Weapons	79
13.	Let It Go	85
14.	You Asked For It	91
15.	Did I Hear You Right	97
16.	It's Available	103
17.	You Are Protected	109
The Provision of God		115
18.	Come On In	119
19.	First Things First	123
20.	Give Him What You Have	129
21.	Rain Or Shine	135
22.	Let Him Use You	139
23.	He Has Something For You	145
24.	What is a Blessing	149
25.	Thank You Lord	155
Conclusion		161
About the Author		169
Upcoming Titles		

The Plan Of God

The elusive plan of God. At least, that is what the world would have you believe about the plan of God. This concept never made sense to me. By the time I became a father, I was over the deep theological concepts of God that were being peddled. As a father, why would I make my kids guess what I wanted or needed from them? Why would I frustrate my children and tell them they need a doctrine degree or a Master's degree to get to know me? Playing guessing games about my plan or purpose doesn't benefit my children or me. If it doesn't benefit me, I know it certainly doesn't benefit God. Like I want and need my children to know me, so does God want and need his children to know him. So, what do we need to know about God? First, God has a plan and purpose; you are included in them. Before we can uncover what they are, it's something significant that you must know about God and his character. If you can understand this one point, you will understand God. If you can grasp this one concept, you can understand the plan of God. Say it slowly. God solves problems! Thats it. That is who he is, and it is also what he does. That isn't all he does, but that is what he wants us to know about him.

God solves problems. From Genesis to Revelations, that is what he does. Genesis chapter one is full of examples of God solving problems. God said let there be light because darkness was a problem. God said, Let us make man after our image and likeness so that man can keep the ground. The man was a solution to a problem. God made Eve because he said it is not good that man should be alone. Eve was a solution to a problem. God sent his only son, Jesus, to solve a problem. The Son of God died to solve a problem. My point is that in everything God does, he does it with the intent to solve a problem. It's no mysteries, no deep secrets; he solves problems. The trouble is that we often don't know the problem he is solving, so we get frustrated. God is a problem solver, and so are you. God strategically made you and sent you here to solve a problem. That is his plan and purpose for your life, but it's up to you if you fulfill it. Either your life is going to solve a problem, or it is going to be a problem. You get to choose.

In creation, one of the first things that God gave man was his image. He made man in his image and after his likeness. It's a little difficult to believe when you look at man's current state and condition. Society has grossly distorted the image of God and the image of the Black man right along with it. Without an accurate representation of God and a true representation of oneself, it leaves a culture and a society in disarray. For any man to be successful, he needs a healthy image of God, himself, and others. How you view these three will ultimately determine your future. So, what is your image of God? What is your image of yourself? What is your image of others? Relying on the world to give you an image of these three things isn't a good plan or option. Yet that is essentially what has happened. If you have the wrong image of something, it brings the wrong expectations. The wrong expectations bring disappointment, mistrust, and misunderstandings. All of this is simply because we have the wrong image. So how do we fix it? What do we do with all of these bad images? The Bible says," Casting down imaginations and every high thing that exalts itself against the knowledge of God "2 Corinthians 10:5. We have gotten into trouble by using our imaginations to create images contrary to God's Word. God wants us to be creative and to use our imaginations but not to create images that corrupt, pollute, and misrepresent who he is.

God gave man a purpose. God gave him a clear-cut assignment because he knew that man would be lost without it. He knew that man not only needed to know what to do, but he also needed to know when to do it. The same need holds true for us today. The struggle has been that instead of knowing the plan and purpose of God, we only had the plan and purpose of men. What was the plan and purpose of men for you? Well, I'll let you fill in the blanks. Black people were brought to this country for what and to do what? The for what was to be slaves. To do what was to work as free labor. I think we all can agree on that. The disagreement comes in on two fronts. Some will tell you it wasn't free labor, but the slave owners provided the other two things that we discuss in this book: that every man needs protection and provisions. I'll discuss both of those later. The second disagreement is whose plan and purpose was it to bring slaves to America? Some argue that it was God's plan and purpose that Black people be enslaved and work for hundreds of years for free. I disagree and say that is a misrepresentation of God. God didn't need slaves to plow his fields or pick his cotton; men did. So, men took their plan and purpose, for Black people wrapped it up in God's name and presented it to Black people. So, if God didn't create Black people to be slaves, then why did he create them? What is his plan? He created them for the purpose that he stated. That they should have dominion, rule, rein, and be fruitful. Sounds familiar? I hope so.

Knowing the plan of God is one of the most powerful things you will ever know. When God gives you power, he will always provide you with a purpose to go with it. Giving you power without purpose is equivalent to giving a toddler car keys. It is dangerous to have power without purpose because it can destroy you and those around you. Within God's plan is hidden your purpose and your power. It has the power to change your life and everyone's life around you. It gives you the ability to move into God's will. Why is that important? Because within God's will, you will have the things you need to reach your full potential. Being within God's will and being outside of God's is the difference between winning and losing. It's the difference between success and failure. This is not only a Biblical principle, but it's a natural principle as well. To illustrate, a palm tree planted in Miami will grow and become beautiful. You can plant that same tree in New York; it would unlikely survive. Most of us are neither planted in New York or Miami, but we abide somewhere in the middle.

Simply put, we aren't necessarily in God's full will, yet we aren't entirely out of it either. We must know His plan to be where he needs us to be. We need to know where He needs us and what he needs us to do. We need to know what to do and when to do it. I know that sounds like a lot to keep track of, but the more often you talk to God, the less information there is to take in. It's like working for a company. Getting a daily report is much less information to digest than getting a monthly report. When you ask God daily what his plan is, you will find the instructions become easier to stay in His will instead of trying to find His will. Now, what is God's plan? The easiest way to see his plans is to look at what He said in His Word.

We live in a world full of information. Some of it is useful, and some of it is not so useful. The valuable information is that which reveals God's plan. All other information is just entertainment, and we are too entertainment-driven. We would rather be entertained than enlightened, but I will discuss that later in the book. We have to shift our value system and reprioritize what is important. The plan of God has to become the most sought-after thing in a man's life. What makes it so valuable is that it contains you and your purpose. Find God's plan and find your purpose. Every man that ever lived will one day sit down and ask himself, "Why am I here, and what is my purpose"? Until a man can answer that question, he will have a void in him. A space that only his purpose can fill. I've seen men try to use money, cars, women, and houses to fill that void. When a man can't fulfill his life with purpose, he fills his life with pleasure as a substitute for his purpose. It always ends the same way. A broken man, breaking things along the way. He is not necessarily breaking things on purpose, but because he neither knows what he is doing nor why he is doing it. The solution is simple. Find the Plan of God, and he will ultimately find the purpose for Himself.

The following nine chapters uncover the plan of God for your life and its importance. Some information will be new to you, and some will probably confirm what you already know. These chapters discuss the basic principles God outlines for us to live by. I call it outline because that is essentially what it is. Think of it as a coloring book. God said you can color your picture with any colors you like, but he has just one rule. Stay within the lines. These chapters will show you where the lines are and how to stay within them.

Chapter One

Dominate Rule Reign And Work

Let them have dominion Genesis 1:26 KJV

Who am I? Why am I here? What is my purpose? Who made me? Where did I come from? Where am I going? These are all valid questions, and life will be difficult if you don't have answers. It's almost like blindfolding someone, dropping them off in a strange county, and then removing the blindfold. That individual will be dazed and confused. From that moment on, they don't function in what they were designed to do; they operate in what they must do. Survival becomes their number one objective. They don't have hopes and dreams because hopes and dreams don't meet the immediate need for food, clothes, or shelter. It's hard to dream of one day owning a restaurant when you don't even have money to eat in one. So, your time is consumed pursuing things instead of dreams. You function in a world of what is needed and not desired. He wonders what he did wrong to be dealt such a cruel and unfortunate hand. Knowing deep down inside that you are better than your circumstances. You know there must be something more significant and better than what you have—knowing it has to be a higher purpose and a higher plan. You are right. There is a higher purpose. So, you start to tackle the hard questions one by one. Who am I? Well, that is a question that no one can answer but you. You define who you are and no one else. You will find that neither your Mother nor your Father can tell you who you are. They can try to help you find yourself, but ultimately, who you are is entirely up to you. If you are a good person, it is because that is what you chose to be. If you are a terrible person, it is because that is what you chose to be. The funny thing is that no one sees themselves as bad, yet we all know some terrible people. Even without a clear definition of good and evil, we can all understand a man's purpose. The answers to who you are is up to you. The answer as to why you are was up to God. The why is easily found in Genesis 1:26, "Then God said let us make man in Our image, according to Our likeness; let them have dominion over the fish of the sea, over the birds of the air, and over the cattle, over the all the earth and over every creeping thing that creeps on the earth." Your purpose and your why are tied up in God's plan. God created you to have dominion over the earth. The word dominion means to dominate. For a man to dominate something, he has to have a domain. A domain is a territory or a colony owned by and ruled by someone. So, God gave man the authority to govern and control the earth. Your purpose is to serve in the governing body that dominates the planet. I phrase it this way because some ethnic groups think they were created to rule over people, not the earth. God never intended for man to rule over each other. He said to rule over the earth and all the beasts of the fields and the fowls of the air, not one another. That helps us see how far we are from God's original plan. God put you here to rule, but not over anyone. He wanted you to reign over things, not people.

Now that we can understand what God said, let's look at why he said it. Why did God give man dominion? God knew that dominion and authority would be necessary for man to complete the assignment God had given him. If we look at Genesis 2:5, it says that the Lord thy God had not caused it to rain upon the earth because it was no man to till the ground. So, God did not allow anything to grow on the earth until he had a man in place to manage it. God is a God of order, and he does not let things grow and then try to figure out later how to manage them. He put the manager in place and allowed things to grow. One of the most important things you can learn is how to manage what God has given you. God will not give according to what you ask for; he will provide you with what he knows you can handle. "To whom much is given, much is required." "If you are faithful over a few things, I will make you ruler over many." These are management principles of God. God created you to be a manager over something. He sent you here to rule and to have dominion in a particular area. It may be a little hard to imagine growing up in a society that often discriminates against you based on your skin color.

Keep in mind that men's sin does not void God's will. If God created you to manage, you will indeed manage. You may not have the title or the recognition that comes with being a manager, but the schemes of men can not revoke the dominion that God gave you. Unfortunately, many of the world's greatest inventions and ideas came directly from people who will never receive credit. They were using their area of dominion. Man can steal your idea, but they can't steal your gift, your ability to manage, or your area of dominion. This explains why God created you and placed you on the earth for a time like this. God created you to solve a problem for your generation. Just as he did with Moses, Joshua, David, and Jesus, they all were born to be a solution, and so were you.

One of the most important texts you will ever read is Titus 1:2. If you need help understanding and believing this one, all other scripture will be hard to grasp. The text gets its value because it says that God cannot lie. It doesn't say He would not lie because that would mean He could have if He had chosen. It says that He cannot lie, which means He couldn't lie even if he wanted. This is important because when you start to doubt His word, this text is your anchor in the storms of life. When questions start to linger in your heart and mind, this scripture will keep everything in perspective.

For this book to do you any good, we must start here. We have to begin with believing everything that God says is true. The reason it is true is that God can't lie. Yes, I will prove that He can't lie and that you can believe what he says. You may not always believe the messenger, but you should always believe the message from God. We all have been lied to and have lied at some point in our lives. Yet, sometimes, we wrongfully equate God with man. God does not need to lie, and He doesn't have the ability to lie. This is important when you start to grasp who God is. We lie out of fear, for self-preservation, and entertainment. God has no fear, and He certainly has nothing to prove, and He is not big on entertaining. It would profit him nothing to deceive anyone with a lie. So, when we consider all the reasons we lie, none are pertinent to God. The ability to lie is one thing we can do that God cannot. To grasp the concept, let's look at why God cannot lie. He is all-powerful and all-knowing; why can't He lie? He cannot lie because He *is* almighty and omnipotent. The word integrity explains who God is.

Integrity means being honest and having moral principles. Also, it is the state of being whole and undivided. God and His word are one. They are whole and undivided. That means what He says and who He is are the same. You cannot separate God's word from Him. God's word is not like our words because His words are impactful. God used His words to frame the world. When God said," Let there be light," there was light. When God said, "Let the light divide the day from the night," so it was. God cannot lie because whatever He says comes to pass. That is why God does not waste words or speak idly. He knows that whatever He speaks will happen and become a reality. In Isaiah 55:11, we read, "So shall my word be that goeth forth out of my mouth: it shall not return unto me void, but it shall accomplish that which I please, and it shall prosper in the thing whereto I sent it." When God speaks, He sends his word out, which goes out with a purpose. That word is heard and heeded by angels. Those angels will go and carry out the words God has spoken. God cannot lie because it's not in Him to lie, and whatever he says will come to pass.

Finding a place to find refuge is challenging in a world full of deception and lies. With all the false information, ads, and broken promises, it's hard not to be a little cynical. When nothing has lived up to the hype or the claims, the perception of the world and God can be distorted, even more so when broken promises come from people from a society that claims to represent God. Incongruent statements include: 'innocent until proven guilty,' 'liberty and justice for all,' 'the right to life, liberty, and the pursuit of happiness,' and 'all men are created equal,' to name a few. These promises are easily made but seldom fulfilled. Many of us will spend our time looking for promises that we should have already obtained. The more one has to fight for these rights, the more the promises feel like lies. The feelings are magnified, especially when you see other ethnic groups exercising these rights that we all have been promised. The truth is that these were rights promised by men who didn't have the authority to make them. If I promised you that I would give you a million dollars, then I need to have a million dollars for the promise to be valid. When this nation makes promises of equality, don't be discouraged. One, you have to know that it is a lie, and two, acknowledge that it won't have the capacity to deliver its promises. God is the only one who can make and keep many of the promises we seek. Only He can assure us of the fulfilled lives we need and desire. Not only will God make us promises, but He also will fulfill them because He cannot lie. So when God said, let them rule and reign over the earth, that is precisely what he intended for us to do. Despite laws and policies designed to rob you of your legal rights, God is still calling and equipping you to dominate.

Dominate, rule, reign, and work. This is your assignment. This entails the reason that God created you and the reason you exist. We often make life more complicated than we should. So, let's keep it simple. Dominate what? The earth. Rule over what? Rule over the fish of the sea, the birds of the air, cattle of the hills, and every creeping thing. Reign over what? Reign over the territory in which God has given you. Work on what? Work in your area of gifting and calling. Work to develop your skills to manage your territory more effectively.

Everyone loves the thought of dominating, ruling, and reigning, but none of that is possible without the work. Your work will determine your ability to dominate, rule, and reign. If you don't put in the work, then don't expect to rule and reign. I promise you that if you work, work will work. To be clear, there is a difference between your work and your job. Your job is what your employer pays you to do, but your work is what you were created to do.

In some cases, you may be fortunate enough that your job and work are the same, but that will only sometimes be the case. Your job is your occupation, but your vocation is your calling. You may be a police officer or truck driver as your occupation, but your vocation may be public speaking or ministry. One is your job, and the other is your calling or work. One is what you chose to do, and the other is what you were created to do. When God told Adam to work, there weren't any jobs or employers. God intended for a man to rule, reign, and dominate the earth. This wasn't man's idea. This was God's plan for man. So, what happens when a man doesn't work or manage the earth? What happens when a man doesn't fulfill his God-given assignment? The world becomes confused and corrupt because no one can keep order. You can't be fruitful and multiply in an overgrown, unkempt jungle. Genesis 2:5 says, "God had not caused it to rain on the earth because there was no man to till the ground." God did not allow anything to grow because there was no manager to manage.

Growth will only happen in areas of your life that you are competent to manage. Don't ask God for things you know you cannot manage. Don't ask for a million dollars if you can't handle a hundred. Don't ask for a house if you can't manage an apartment. It's always appropriate to ask God to help you better manage your time, talent, and resources. That is a prayer request that God is always honored to answer. He will gladly help us to become better managers of the earth. When we try to fulfill his vision for the earth and not ours, we can live an abundant life.

I don't want anyone to be naïve and believe that just because you have this God-given assignment, the devil will be okay with you dominating the earth. The devil has been doing all he can to keep you from ruling in your area of dominion. He has enslaved you, physically and mentally, to believe that you are not qualified to rule. He has made it culturally and socially unacceptable for you to have dominion or authority. Whether through laws or discriminatory practices, it is clear that the devil has an issue with your reigning. This is not my perception or my opinion. It is a historical fact. Even if you are the most knowledgeable or qualified in your area of dominion, you will still have to overcome unjust oppression. If you can name another ethnic group that has been more oppressed, displaced, discriminated against, and mistreated than the black race, I would love to hear about them. The debate isn't about did it indeed happen. The discussion is about why it happened and why it still happens. Why does the devil do so much to oppose one group of people? Why does the devil have so much hate, animosity, and disdain towards Black People? He hasn't done half the things to any other ethnic group he has to Black people. He has enslaved, raped, mutilated, displaced, discriminated, and experimented on one group of people. Why? Yes, the devil hates everyone, but he has a different level of hate for Black people. He has a disdain for Black people that is unsurpassed and unlike anything that has ever been seen worldwide. I challenge you to think about it because the why becomes very clear if you think about it. The devil hates us because he knows that if the Black man dominates, rules, and reigns in the earth, the earth will look how God intended it to look. The Black man has the mental, physical, and spiritual capacity to make the world look like God intended for it to look. That's why he hates us. When Black people function in their area of dominion, rule, and reign, it is a reflection of the love and compassion that God intended to share within the earth. We are some of the most loving, forgiving, and compassionate people on the planet. What would it look like if those types of people ran your government? What would it look like if those types of people ran your business? What would it look like if those types of people ran your community? I'm referring to those who are doing the work and are enlightened about their purpose—those who understand what has happened and why. God has given man dominion, and he will not take it back. The question is, what are we going to do with it?

Chapter Two

Don't Waste Your Time

Remember now thy Creator in the days of thy youth, while the evil days come not. Ecclesiastes 12:1, KJV

Who is the poorest man on earth? It's not the man who doesn't have money but the man who doesn't have time. If you have enough time, you can eventually do anything. You could subsequently earn over a million dollars if you have enough time. If you start to work at age twenty-five, making thirty thousand dollars a year, and work until you are sixty-five, you would have earned $1,200,000 in your lifetime. That is if you have the time.

It's better for a person to rob you of your possessions than to rob you of your time. You can replace your possessions, but your time is irreplaceable. Learn what makes you valuable. Some people will hate you because of your color, and others might despise you because of your youth. Let that sink in. They will try to rob you of your time and youth, and it's people who usually do not have as much time as you, so they try to shorten yours. Sending you away for years for petty crimes will rob you of your youth. They want to rob you because they know you are rich, and I need you to know you are rich, too. I promise they will trade all their money in exchange for your youth.

Being young is one thing that we tend to take for granted. We take youth for granted because we have never experienced what it is like to get old. For the most part, we can perform a task without help or assistance. We can rise or lie down at will. This Scripture reminds us that it will not always be this way. Growing up is as much part of life as living itself. There's no way around it. I don't think that we intentionally take our youth for granted, but I believe we have a poor concept of time when we are young. We spend time without real thought about its value and our inability to get it back. So what should we do? First, make sure you live your life in a manner that will allow you to get old. Don't participate in or condone risky behavior. You have to realize that society views you differently from how it views your peers. You will not be afforded different chances that other cultures have. Your mistakes will be magnified and may even shorten your life span or freedom. You live in a country that does not value your life as much as it does others, so you must ensure that you love and value your own life. You can't expect society to value you when you don't even value yourself. You have to feel that your life is worth too much to throw it away and waste it. To truly understand your value, you must know what makes you valuable. Your worth isn't measured in cars, clothes, or homes. Your weight isn't measured in possessions or accolades. Your value is measured in purpose.

You were born with a purpose and for a purpose. That is what makes you valuable. God did not send you here to go out to find your purpose; he sent you with a built-in purpose and drive. All you have to do is let your purpose out. God took a purpose and an assignment, wrapped you around it, and sent you into the world to fulfill your purpose, not to find it. When you go out into the world to find your purpose, the world will give you one that is not yours. The world will provide you with a purpose that fits its needs and not your own. They try to make you become things that God never intended for you to become. Prime example: God never intended that you become a slave. Well, not you, but your ancestors. The world took people and gave them a purpose that suited their needs. God didn't need slaves; the Colonizers did. The Colonizers also tried to convince the slaves for over 400 years that their enslavement was within God's will. That shows you how dangerous it can be not knowing God's will and plan. You have to resist the urge to be what the world wants you to be and become that in which God has made *you*.

I stated that your purpose is within you, and you must let it out. To illustrate further, Prince Rogers Nelson was one of the greatest musicians ever. 'Prince' didn't go out in the world to find music; music was already in Prince. He just went into the world to show what was in him. Michael Jordan didn't go into the world to find basketball; basketball was already in him. A comedian does not go into the world to learn how to be funny or to tell jokes. Jokes are already in him. My point is these people had gifts and purpose, and they showed us the talents and purpose that God had hidden within them. Sometimes, our gifts are buried so far underneath jobs, relationships, or family responsibilities that we can't identify them.

God has given you gifts and purpose, and we are waiting for the manifestation of your purpose. Show us why you are here. The Scripture reminds us to 'remember thy Creator in the days of (y)our youth. That means that your youth is the time to develop your gift and fulfill your purpose. That doesn't mean that if you are older, that your purpose is done. It means don't waste your life doing things that are not a part of your purpose. At some point, God will ask you if you fulfilled your purpose and what you did with the gifts He gave you. The world is designed to make you forget your purpose and Creator. It would have you only live for today. Don't fall into the trap of thinking that your gifts will always be there and your purpose will wait for you. When you are young and robust, devote your energy to the Creator's plan and purpose for your life. Don't wait until you are old and feeble to remember your Creator. He has plans for you today!

The text says to remember your Creator in the days of your youth. Part of the problem is that we can't remember a Creator we never knew. It's like me telling you to remember a song you have never heard or a book you have never read. To remember something, you must have been exposed to what it is you should remember. There was a time during which, even if we did not belong to a church, we had spent a significant amount of time hearing about God. That is not so much the case today. We attended church with our grandparents, aunts, uncles, neighbors, and friends. We were in the car or on the bus with anyone attending church. In the summer months, we attended church camps and Vacation Bible School. Today's society has fallen away from this type of instruction and familiarity with the Creator. The result is we have whole generations that have not even been exposed to God, so how can they remember a God Whom we have failed to teach them about? We have a two-part problem. One, we need teachers willing to teach, and two, students ready to learn. Then, we will be able to remember our Creator in the days of our youth.

If you already know God, continue growing and developing your relationship with Him. If you don't know God, today is the day to get to know Him. God wants nothing in the world more than a deeper relationship with you. He wants you to understand what he can do and who He is. Knowing God can remove a lot of frustration from your life. You are no longer guessing or wandering through life from one bad situation to another. You can have your own personal GPS that will tell you which way to go and where to turn. If you ever find yourself in a situation where you don't know where to go or what to do, as the text says, "Remember thy Creator in the days of thy youth." Don't waste your time. You can't afford it.

Chapter Three

A Changed Mind Equals A Changed Man

AND BE NOT CONFORMED TO THIS WORLD: BUT BE YE TRANSFORMED BY THE RENEWING OF YOUR MIND. ROMANS 12:2, KJV

Every man enters this world as a blank slate or an empty canvas. Every day, someone will take their paintbrush and place a stroke of paint on the canvas of your mind. With each stroke, you will form pictures and ideas that collaborate with your experiences and those you allow into your life. Before long, you have a complete portrait of events and images created by the hands of your environment and any preconceived ideas you may have. You will find that some people in your life will make beautiful strokes with bold colors and dazzling designs that enhance your life. At the same time, others will paint ugly scars that limit your creativity and stifle your potential and desire for greatness.

Two forces are painted on the same canvas: good and evil. How do you think the portrait will come out? Will it be beautiful to the point that the world will be amazed at its glory? Or will it be a vile disaster that no one wants to behold or be forced to look at? The truth is in life, there will probably be both. There will be beautiful seasons, but there will also be seasons in which it will be very unattractive. What will determine the outcome of the seasons will be *you*. It all depends on which artist you allow to paint on your canvas. It depends on which one you are willing to dedicate most of your time to and to decide with whom you spend your time.

In this life, we have dueling artists competing for studio time in our minds. Both of them desire to get in and create, but it's entirely up to you who you allow in. Neither can force their way in, but one is more deceptive. They both appear good, but unfortunately, they are hard to tell apart. Sometimes, the only way to tell them apart is to allow them to start painting. It will take more than one or two strokes to tell the difference between them. The portrait may almost be complete before you can identify the actual artist. Is it God, or is it the devil?

There will come a day when you realize there were people who meant well but didn't necessarily do well. In other words, they told you things you later discovered weren't true, and neither were they helpful! There are many people with good intentions painting bad portraits. It may be a parent, teacher, or even a pastor. Nevertheless, God has a solution to your problem. God said, "Be not conformed to this world, but be ye transformed by the renewing of your mind." The beautiful thing about renewing your mind is that you can do it at any age. You can be young and robust or old and feeble, but your mind will determine your path.

First, you must know that people will always try to sell you something or another. There are people whose job is to convince you to try something or to buy something. Advertisements are everywhere, and depending on where you live will usually determine if they are good or evil. Pay attention the next time you visit the store and see what is advertised. As you drive along, look at the signs and see how many things are on billboards that will make your life better. Then, when you arrive at your local convenience store, what is advertised in the window? Is it bread, milk, Gatorade, beer, wine, or cigarettes? I'm bringing this to your attention because if you can tell what is being advertised, I can tell you what side of town you are without ever having been there. Indeed, that is possible because of someone's intentions. Someone has thoroughly planned out where to advertise specific ideas and products. After years of this influence, you become programmed to accept certain things. It becomes customary to you, and you don't even pay it any attention. Eventually, you conform to the thought process and images you have allowed them to paint in your mind. Thankfully, God has to intervene and challenge the portraits you have become comfortable seeing.

God said to be not conformed to this world but be ye transformed. You will never change your life until you first let God change your mind. He won't force you, but he will allow life to get hard to help you see that your way of thinking does not work. God will allow you to come to your wit's end. When you run out of plots, schemes, and plans, God will show you His. Too often, we must be backed into a corner before we are willing to listen to what God has to say. We are so accustomed to taking everyone's advice but God's. The reason is that often, God's advice doesn't make sense to us. God will give you instructions contrary to what the world says: not for Him to test you, but for you to test Him. God wants you to know that you can trust Him, and He doesn't mind proving Himself. God is saying He will change your life, but first, He must change your mind.

Why does God have to change your mind? God has to change your mind before He changes your life because if He doesn't, your life will return to the way it was before. The thinking that got you where you are will ultimately lead you back if God doesn't deal with it. So, God says be not conformed to this world but be ye transformed by the renewing of your mind.

How do you renew an old mind? How do you transform a mind full of concepts, ideas, and principles? You transform a mind by spending time with God. The same way you change your body by going to the gym. The same way weights and treadmills transform the body is the same way God's word changes the mind. When you pray, read, and study God's word, it becomes the ultimate transformation tool. There is no better way to get to know a person than spending time with them. The more time that you spend with God, the better you will know Him, and the better you know Him, the better your life will be.

Conforming to this world is a process that only happens over time; therefore, transforming your mind will also take time. You think the way you think because you have years of programming. Years of television, billboards, and advertisements have programmed you to feel the way you do. It was a process. Transforming your mind will also be a process, but the process that God will use will be different. He is not going to bombard you with annoying ads or catchphrases. He is going to use the revelation of simple truth and his word. The manifestation of His unconditional love and never-ending dedication to your well-being will change your mind and heart.

Renewing your mind will be the most significant change you can make and one of the most fulfilling. When God changes your mind, He will then take responsibility for the decisions that you make. You can rest well and have confidence in the choices that you make. One of the most incredible benefits isn't knowing the results or the outcomes since you still may not know either, but it is knowing whose instructions you follow. You can have peace when you know what you desire and compare it to what God instructed you to do—knowing this wasn't your plan or idea. Frequently, God's plan is more than you can think of or imagine. The gap between what God thinks and the way we believe is so vast that it is described in Isaiah 55:9: "As the heavens are higher than the earth, so are My ways higher than your ways, and My thoughts are higher than your thoughts." For us to be effective in life, God has to elevate our minds. That includes all of us, whether we have been walking with God all our lives or are newly acquainted with Him. The result is peace from knowing that God changed our minds. The peace from a changed mind isn't always external but internal. Most of the time, chaos will surround you, but peace will be all within you. Friends and family may struggle to understand your new attitude and way of thinking. They may question your intent and even your character in some cases. Within you, the choice and pathway may be clear to you but cloudy to others. When these situations arise, it's essential to remain humble at all times. Never forget that there was a time in your life when, if God had not changed your mind, you would still be walking in darkness. We still have areas God is trying to change our minds about. Just as God gives us time to change our minds, we have to allow God time to change other's minds, too. Remember, if the choice is whether to be humble or right, always choose to be humble. None of us can always be right, but we can always be humble. Learning how to travel on the road of humility on the way to being right shortens our travel back to humility for the times in which we are wrong. Traveling the road of humility also covers you if, when you get to the end of the road, it reveals you were wrong. Life will teach us much more in the times that we are wrong than it ever will during the times that we are right. Being right doesn't teach you very much. It only confirms what you already know, but being wrong reveals an opportunity to grow. Everyone can see the value in being right, but when you arrive at a point in life where you can see the value of being wrong, you are on your way to greatness. Being wrong is an opportunity to change and grow. Being wrong isn't a travesty. Being wrong and choosing to stay wrong is a travesty. God wants to teach us something by changing our minds. If he doesn't teach, it's on him. If we choose not to learn, it's on us.

Chapter Four

See You At the Finish Line

For I know the thoughts that I think towards you, saith the Lord, thoughts of peace and not evil, to give you an expected end. Jeremiah 29:11, KJV

One of the worst things you can believe is that you were an accident and not planned. God did not set you up for failure. He did not create and place you in a body with dark skin to curse or punish you. He didn't make you dark so that you would be less educated, less important, or less informed than other races. He didn't make you dark so others could identify who would become servants and those who would be their masters. God didn't make you dark to curse you, but he made you dark to bless you. If you happen to be white, He didn't make you white to curse or condemn you. God chose for all of us as to our ethnicity and the color of our skin where we live our lives. He made us according to His plan and not according to ours. Although God knew how we would treat and view each other, God still created us differently from one another. He could have made us all the same color and race, but He had a plan for something greater. God wanted a family that was just as diverse as He. God is and always will be more than we can imagine. When we define Him as possessing a particular skin color or race, we limit Him. We limit His ability to understand and empathize with us. So, no race or person can accurately portray all He is outside of Jesus Christ. That's why we are many members of one body.

God has an opinion about you! " He has an opinion on where you should live, work, worship, and attend school." He even has an opinion on what you should eat and how you should dress. God cares very much about where and how we live. Even though He has thoughts and ideas, He will never override your freedom to choose. God will never force you to adhere to His opinion. He won't even make you listen if you don't want to hear his opinion.

For years, society taught us and led us to believe that God didn't care about us. The message was that He doesn't care about our living conditions, but He does care about our moral condition. This message is hypocritical in every sense of hypocrisy. To not care about someone's living condition but then pass judgment on someone's moral condition is a misrepresentation of God. In other words, if we had an earthly father who didn't love us enough to ensure we ate, how could he chastise us for stealing food? After all, if he had provided for us, we wouldn't have to resort to stealing. We can't blame God for this because this wasn't the message from God or his Son. The message was from those who claimed to represent God under the banner of Christianity and a nation that portrays itself as a Christian nation. The

Country can describe itself as anything it likes, but it is revealed under close examination. It's easier to play the role of a Christian nation than to be one. Remember that the Klu Klux Klan and White Nationalists see themselves as Christian organizations. This kind of portrayal of God has had a devastating effect on Black people. It has held you mentally, physically, and spiritually bound. People have pointed out our status and tried to use it as a measurement tool to demonstrate our "importance to God. They said," We have less because "we were less, which was how God intended." The lies that we have been led to believe have no limit.

The truth is that God cares about us as well as the choices that we make. God cares about our needs and our desires. He cares about the paths that we travel and our overall well-being. He cares more than we could imagine. Too often, we think God is like many others we have encountered. He only cares if it benefits Him, but God cares for no other reason than he loves us. Not only does He love us, but He loves us enough to have plans for our lives.

God created you to be born for a time such as this. He allowed you to be here at this time and this season to accomplish great things. You are not too early, and neither are you too late. You are in the right place at the right time. God carefully planned out the days of our lives and the things in it.

This scripture says that He knows the thoughts He has toward you. That means He doesn't have to rely on you and doesn't need anyone to give Him an opinion about you. He doesn't have to ask family or neighbors about you. He doesn't have to rely on social media or news outlets. He already has his thoughts and opinions about you, and no one helped Him form it. God knows your successes and failures; no man had to familiarize Him with them. Finally, don't waste your time trying to obtain favor with a man or with the world when you already have favor with God. God has placed favor on your life if you follow the path that He has laid. If God places your blessings along Interstate 20 and you choose to travel on Interstate 65, who can you blame if you do not have what you need? You can't make your plan and path and expect God to move the blessing to where you are. The blessings are on the path He planned for your life, and it's up to you to follow it. God has a plan to bless you, but do you plan to receive it? If not, that may be why you have yet to receive it. If God thinks enough to plan how and where He will bless you, is it requiring too much of you to plan how and where you will *receive* it? Here is where we miss it. There are plans and purposes for you, and there are also plans and purposes for the blessings. God has given much thought to them both. We should consider daily "What's the plan"? We should start our day with the mindset of, 'Okay, Lord, 'what is the plan and purpose for the day?

God is the Quarterback and calling the plays, but many of us keep running the wrong routes. He's not going to change the plays because He has a plan. You have to change your route. The blessings will be there if you run the plays and routes He calls. God will read the defense and make an audible at the line of scrimmage, and He will take what the defense gives Him. We must trust God to call the plays that will get us the victory." Don't just run where you think you should run. Run to the places that God would have you run. When He draws up the plays, He draws them up with us in mind, but we have to be in the huddle to get the play. When the basketball coach calls a timeout, He calls all the players over to the bench, drawing up the play. How can you know the play if you don't come to the huddle and stand at half-court? Not only do you not know the play, but you also hinder those who do. You interfere and take up space for those who are in place. The huddle is prayer. Prayer is where you huddle with God, and you get the play, you get the instructions, and you ask questions. In prayer, you discover, 'Who is there to block for you'? Who is there to pass you the ball, and to whom you can pass it back? Who is there to 'set you a pick' and who is there to 'give you an assist?

All of this is made known in the huddle. This is why the devil hates prayer, and even more so does he hate corporate prayer. When we all huddle up and pray, the coach says that he will be one in the midst. The text says, "I know the thoughts that I think towards you," said the Lord, thoughts of peace and not of evil. You have to trust the Play-Caller. He sees the whole field. So when God is trying to bless us and give us an expected end, that only can happen if we run the correct route and are in a position to receive what God is throwing our way.

If you have ever wondered what is on God's mind and what He is thinking about, it's you. He constantly thinks about you and how he can bring you to an expected end. If we can learn to travel along the pathway that God has planned for us, we can have an abundant life. We have to know that the devil is trying to draw us off the path every day. He places cars, houses, and even women just in view to lure you off the path. It's like trying to walk to catch a setting sun. If you start to walk toward the sun while it is setting, at first, it appears like you are getting closer. In reality, you are not getting closer; you are just getting farther off the path. By the time you realize where you are, not only will you have not caught the sun, but it will leave you in darkness. Life is full of distractions, and I wish there were a cure for them, but it's not. It's not a cure, but there are ways to deal with them. Where you are going should always be more important than where you are. Always be grateful for what you have; know someone would love to be in your shoes. Know that there are no shortcuts in life, only deadends that appear to be a faster route.

Remember, there is a finish line, even if you can't see it. No matter how old or young you may be, there is a finish line for all of us. This thing we call today will be tomorrow in less than 24 hours. We all are only born with a limited amount of tomorrow's. Don't waste your today counting on your tomorrow. One of the greatest quotes I've ever heard goes like this: "You will never reach your destination if you stop to throw a rock at every barking dog." In other words, don't waste your time; you have somewhere to be, and most dogs you will encounter are as far as they will ever go. They are stuck at the fence, watching you pass by. If it's not blocking your path, it's not essential. See you at the finish line.

Chapter Five

Trust the Process

AND WE KNOW THAT ALL THINGS WORK TOGETHER FOR GOOD, TO THEM THAT LOVE GOD TO THEM THAT ARE THE CALLED ACCORDING TO HIS PURPOSE. ROMANS 8:28 KJV

Life is a puzzle, and often, we struggle to put it together. We need pieces or need help figuring out how they fit together. When unforeseen circumstances or events occur, we must remember that God is trying to get us somewhere important. Where? To Heaven. That is the most important thing in the world to God: one day, we can be reunited with Him forever in eternity. I said this to help you understand how far God will go to make this happen. While He is not willing to force anyone who doesn't want to go, He is willing to do whatever it takes to save those of us who do. God can help us understand that everything that happens to us is not all good but always for our good. That is why trusting Him is so important. It's easy to trust Him when things go our way, but can you trust Him when things are not to our liking?

God's ultimate goal is to get His children home, and in the process, there will be some good and bad times. There will be some heartache and pain. When difficult times come, remember that where you are going is more important than where you are. During difficult times, God is closest to us. God will use the storms of life to remove some things, but He will also use the storms of life to bring us some things. Some people would have never left your life had there not been storms. God uses storms to uncover who is really rooted and grounded in your life. There are things and people that God wants to remove from you, so He will use storms to blow them away. Yet, God will use the same wind that blew some things away from you to blow some new things into your life. We can't appreciate what is coming when we focus too much on the things and people who left.

Remember, all things work together for the good; not all things are good, but they all work together. That's why it is so important to keep a grateful heart. The most challenging things in life can be some of the greatest blessings. In difficult situations, remember they, too, have a purpose. Even Judas, who betrayed Jesus, was necessary. So are friends and family who betray you. When the doctor gives you bad news, when you get fired from the job you loved, when you lose all your possessions, God is still God. Your situation doesn't make him any more or less God. When a loved one dies and goes to heaven. Remember, all things are working together for your good. God knew these things would happen, but most importantly, He knew how you would react to them. Don't allow life to make you forget who you are. You are the call of God, according to His purpose. That means that you did not choose God, but God chose you. He desires you to represent Him in whatever you are going through and dealing with. If you were born with a lot or without anything at all, God chose you because He knew you could handle it. God puts a lot on you because He knows He put a lot in you. He will not demand anything from you that He didn't first put in you. If it seems God is placing demands on your forgiveness, it's because He knows that he put forgiveness in you. If it looks like He demands your time or talent, it is only because He knows how much time and talent he has given you. If He places demands on your finances, it's because He knows how much you can afford.

When you were born, God deposited many things in you. He gave you intelligence, reasoning, feelings, wisdom, discernment, love, and talent. He sent you into the world with the necessary amount of funds to successfully return home. Don't become angry or frustrated with life when it demands that you produce what God has deposited in you. In banking terms, when you enter the bank, they will use something the bankers call a banker's draft. A banker's draft is like asking a bank to write a check for you. This banker's draft is called a cashier's check. You give them the funds, and the financial institution issues a check for you in the amount you give them. This check ensures the check does not 'bounce' for a lack of funds. Take heart! Don't become discouraged when life demands you pay upfront because God has already made a transaction that cannot and will not bounce. Regardless of the withdrawal amount, God has already covered the draft. He has already installed in you enough of everything you need to be what He has called you to be. You have to allow Him to make the withdrawal. You already have enough love, faith, patience, knowledge, and wisdom within you to handle everything that life throws at you.

When the God of Creation began to create the world, He did something unique in chapter one of Genesis. He created some things and other things he called forth. He created the dry land and called the grass and trees to come out of the dry land. He created the sea and then called the sea to bring forth the fish, the birds, and other living creatures. He created these things and then called forth the items He had placed in them. The revealing of these things to us portrays the glory of God.

Similarly, everything within us has not yet been revealed when God created you and me. In the right season, God will call forth the things He has placed in us to display his glory. Often, a problem or an issue that will arise in our lives will cause God to command things to, 'Come forth.' That's when we will produce the thing God has hidden in us that will bring Him glory. The next time you think you are challenged beyond your limits, I urge you to look inside yourself. Look and see what has yet to be revealed. Know that "All things work together for good to them that love God, to them who are the called according to His purpose." God has called you and Also called you for a purpose and created you with a purpose.

Don't become frustrated in the process. Your purpose in life may not have been revealed yet, but it will be. The fact that you are still here lets us know that your purpose has not yet been fulfilled. The enemy plans to get you to abandon God's purpose for your life. While it is, indeed, the enemy that holds us back sometimes, it is also us holding ourselves back. We sometimes have made plans and dreams that don't align with God's plans. If there are two plans, one must fail so the other may succeed. Only God can take the things we thought to be failures and turn them into successes. God can turn the things we count as evil into blessings. God cannot only make *some* things work in our favor, but He can make *all* things work in our favor. Even the things that we'd rather not deal with or accept. When you allow all things to work together, God will make them work out in your favor. Trusting the process has to become a part of our daily routine. When you wake up in the morning, you should be excited to know that something is about to happen on this day for your good. As you venture out into the world, you should seek the good things God has promised. Keep in mind it might not be the whole thing all at once. It may only be a piece of pie and not the whole pie. If God said he would bless you with a home, he may give it to you one brick at a time and not all at once. What seems even more fascinating is that those bricks may be the ones your enemies throw at you. God can use the things the enemy designed to hurt us to help us, but it largely depends on our attitudes toward life.

We all will experience some pain and disappointment in life. Life will deal us all a bad hand if you sit down at the table long enough. Many people throw in the towel and quit because they get a bad hand. They clearly aren't the spades players that I grew up with. One of the things that separates good spades players from great ones is how they handle their bad hands. A great spades player takes pride in being able to take nothing and turn it into something. He isn't moved when he gets a bad hand because he knows that even with a bad hand, he will get the most out of what he was dealt. He knows that a bad hand is a part of the game and is not personal. Most of all, he knows if he can just hold on and make it through, another hand is coming. He knows it will take more than a bad hand to make him quit. His confidence isn't in the cards or the dealer. His confidence is in his ability to play the game. He thinks back on all the times that he was able to overcome a bad hand and how he was still able to win. This should be the confidence that every child of God has. They should know not just in their head but in their heart that they were built to win. So even when it looks like they are losing, they are still winning because all things work together for good, to them that love God to them that are called according to his purpose.

Chapter Six

You Owe Them

HONOR THY FATHER AND MOTHER; WHICH IS THE FIRST COMMANDMENT WITH A PROMISE. EPHESIANS 6:2 KJV

Several scripture passages are similar to the one found in Ephesians, but they all convey the same message. That message is the expectations God has on how we treat our parents. It can be challenging for many Black men without looking at the culture because the families and the homes have often been torn apart for various reasons. Most of our relationships with one or, in some cases, both parents have been strained. Whether that parent has chosen to be absent or not, the instruction from God remains the same. Whether that parent is missing due to divorce, separation, incarceration, abandonment, death, or willful neglect, we are still faced with the same instruction to honor them.

To honor your father and mother, you must first know what it means to honor. Honor goes much further than Mother's Day and Father's Day gifts. It's not just referring to flowers on Mother's Day and ties on Father's Day. It goes beyond mere lip service. Honoring your parents has to become a lifestyle, not just an occasion. That means day in and day out, you live your life in a manner that will not bring shame or disgrace to your parent's name. We don't truly understand the value of having someone's name because the names that we were given were not ours due to slavery. We don't have a long history that we can look back on and say that our family made significant achievements to be proud of. By nature, we undervalue our namesake—not realizing that survival within itself was an outstanding achievement for our parents and grandparents. Therefore, we think little about how our actions affect our parents' names when we enter the world. We don't ask our parents if they want their name associated with lying, stealing, or crime. We don't ask them if they want to be known as the parent of a drug dealer, alcoholic, or addict. Not realizing that if they wanted their names associated with any of those things, they could have done it themselves. We make decisions and feel like we don't owe anything to the people who made us possible. When God said honor thy father and mother, it goes beyond just birth parents. Father and Mother are whoever had the task of raising and providing you with food and taking care of your needs."

I'm sure that we all have disagreements with our parents on issues. A conflict does not mean you dishonor your parents, nor does it mean you are disrespecting them. There is a way to disagree with your parents and still honor them. You can have a different opinion and differ on an issue from your parents and still honor them. Remember that honoring them doesn't necessarily mean that they are right or that you agree with them, but it does mean that you agree that God is right.

After all, He didn't say honor your father and mother because they are right. God said to honor them because of who they are. Even if you have a hard time doing it because of who they are, do it because of who He is. Honor them because He is God, and you choose to honor Him as such. No, your parents may not deserve to be honored, but you still should do it because God deserves to be honored. Do it to make sure you stay in a proper relationship with God. Do it because your life is also a reflection of Him.

Sadly, some of us have fathers and mothers we don't know. They have played little or no role in our lives. Yet, these circumstances do not negate the word of God. This scripture does not have a disclaimer saying, 'You are only to honor those parents which deserve honor.' He said, 'Honor thy father and thy mother.' This passage doesn't affect how you feel about them or how they have treated you.

At this point, the only question remains, 'What does honor look like'? It can vary significantly from culture to culture and home to home. So, when God tells us to honor our parents, what should we do? I think it is easier to explain what we should *not* do.

Your name is significant. Your name will be the way that the world will identify you. They will use your name to identify who you are and what you are. With your name, there also comes responsibility. You also carry that name in every act you commit, and everywhere you go. If you ascend to great heights, you have that name; however, if you descend to the lowest of lows, you carry that name. You and only you will ultimately define that name you bear. It will be known for the acts and deeds of your parents and the deeds you commit. Your community will be shaped and molded by your choices and decisions. The way they will identify who has done good or bad will be in the name you have carried.

So, you honor your father and mother by how you carry your name. I don't want you to think you are exempt if your last name differs from your parents. You still honor them the same way. You can have a different last name, but I assure you that people still know whose child you are. You still reflect your parents, even if your last name differs. Even more, in a society that doesn't know God, they still know to whom you belong. Therefore, to honor your parents, there have to be some things you will not do because you do not want to dishonor your parent's names. There must be some rules you will not break, not because doing so would reflect on you, but because doing so would also reflect on your parents.

You respected your teachers in school because your actions reflected your parents' values. In society, you respect your co-workers because doing so reflects your parents' values. You honor your parents by avoiding things that will bring them shame and not doing something that will bring them dishonor.

The great thing about honoring your parents is that you do not do it in vain. God has said that this is the first commandment with a promise if you honor them. What is that promise? "That thing will be well with thee, and thou may live long upon the earth." If things are not 'going well with you,' make sure you live a lifestyle that honors your parents. If you are struggling in life, make sure that you are not carrying bitterness or resentment toward your parents. God has promised that things will be well if you honor your parents. When trouble arises, you can sleep well. You know that God has you because you have done what he asked. When things threaten your peace of mind, find refuge, knowing God has promised you a long life on earth.

This scripture is essential for you to know because the devil knows it. He knows that if he can cause enough discord between parents and their children, he can destroy the children. So much tension exists in homes, and it's not by accident. The devil tries daily to make children dishonor their parents to shorten their lifespans. It's a trap, and many people fall into it, not knowing it's all a part of the devil's plan. Thankfully, there are steps that we can take to avoid falling into this trap, but the foremost one is to know the scripture and apply it. Have a made-up heart and mind that you would never dishonor your parents. If you do find yourself in this situation, stop. You may even have to put some distance between you and that parent, but it's better to be apart with honor than together with dishonor.

Another aspect we must consider is that we commonly honor one parent and dishonor the other. In some cases, one parent may promote or even encourage the children to dishonor another if the relationship between the two parents is bad. This is a terrible and dangerous game to play. God said to honor thy father and mother, not just the one you like or agree with. He also didn't say we don't have to honor the other parent if one of them says it is okay. I know it is a challenging situation to be in, but we still know right from wrong. It is unfortunate to be in a situation where the parents try to make the children choose sides, but I have a solution. Choose God's side. If a parent tells or encourages you to disrespect the other, I strongly suggest disobeying. Any parent that does that or suggests that isn't the best person to get advice from. While it may make it harder for you and that parent to get along with, I would rather struggle with a relationship with a parent than my relationship with God.

Parents have been known to carry grudges and hostilities toward each other that existed even before you were born. It is by no means your job to carry out the vendetta that they started with one another before you were even born in some cases. You can respectfully tell that parent what you are doing and why you are doing it. You can say I'm choosing to honor my father and mother because that is what God requires of me. You don't just owe one of your parents honor; you owe it to both. Even if you don't receive the same honor back from them, you have done your part. God isn't going to ask you what kind of parents you had. He will ask you what kind of child you were to your parents. I've seen a lot of parent-child relationships both at the beginning and the end of life. I've never seen a child regret honoring their parents at the graveside, but I've seen many children wishing they had honored their parents while they had them. Pay them honor. Trust me, it's a lot cheaper to pay them honor than it is to pay them what we owe.

Chapter Seven

Count up the Cost

Husbands love your wives, just as Christ also loved the church and gave himself for her. Ephesians 5:25 KJV

Many men marry in hopes of what they wish to receive, but being a husband is more about what the Husband is ready to give. Being a husband requires that you be prepared to be a constant giver. With that in mind, if you are selfish, you may want to think long and hard before you say, "I do." Becoming a husband demands that you be ready to give all you have and some things you don't. How can you share something that you do not have? You have to go out and get them or be willing to allow someone else to give them. Therefore, being a husband will be challenging if you are proud or require recognition for your accomplishments or actions. Few tasks require more humility than those of a husband. You will fail publicly and privately and must be okay with that.

Every man should count up the cost before he gets married and see if he can afford to be a husband. I said he needs to know if he can afford "to be a husband" and not "to get married." The cost is different. There's minimal cost associated with getting married. If you have the money for the marriage license, they will undoubtedly give you one, but to be a husband is much more costly. Being a husband will cost you time, money, friends, family, hobbies, and patience. You should count those things to see if you can afford to be a husband. I don't bring up these things to discourage you, but I bring them up to inform you. Countless books and resources are available to help you determine if you are ready to become a husband. Don't be too proud to use them.

God set a standard for the husband, and it's non-negotiable. I did not specify the standard, nor did I even take part in defining the standard, but God Himself described what a husband should and shouldn't be. These standards were set to create stability in the home and for the family. God never intended that a husband and wife separate because He intended everyone to do their part. If you are a husband or thinking about becoming one, you should find out what your part is. Getting married and not being aware of your responsibilities is like taking a job and not knowing the duties. If you are unemployed, you may accept whomever will hire you without knowing your responsibilities. All you want is a check or income. Yet, if you find out that the pay is too little or the work is too hard, you will eventually quit. The same holds true when it comes to being a husband. If all you wanted were to be married and found that the work was too hard or the pay was too little, you would also quit your marriage.

When God created marriage, He made it to be a solution to a problem. He didn't just devise an idea that He would institute marriage. He was trying to solve something. God had something on His mind, and if you have something different in mind from what God had, you are on the wrong track. Your marriage is either going to solve a problem, or it is going to be a problem. The outcome is determined by how well you know and perform your job.

You and your spouse should carry out your marriage so that generations will look at it and say they want what you have. You should be the kind of Husband that when young men see you, they should want to become husbands. Your conduct as a husband should be such that young women wish to have a husband with a character and ways similar to yours. How can you make this happen? By following the instructions:

Ephesians 5:25 says, "Husbands love your wife as Christ loved the church and gave himself for it." Do you love the woman enough to give yourself for her? In other words, do you love her enough to die for her? To keep it in context, I asked if you loved her enough to die for her, not enough to allow her to kill you. I said this because I have seen some wonderful husbands who married terrible wives. You can lay down your life for your wife as Christ laid his down for the church, but he didn't allow the church to kill him. You must know the difference. A good wife will not let her Husband kill himself. A good wife will not even allow you to harm yourself. I've seen men who work several jobs, cook, clean, and care for the children, and it's still not enough for some wives. This Husband isn't laying down his life for his wife; he is allowing his wife to kill him. If doing these things brings the husband joy, then, by all means, have at it. Yet, if it breaks the Husband down mentally, spiritually, and physically, and the wife does not intervene, she is killing him.

Husbands, your responsibility is to love your wives. That means that you protect, provide, and care for her. Sometimes, this may be more difficult than other times. In those times, you must know Who gave you the assignment of loving her. Your marriage will cost you more love, money, time, and patience than you have. In those times, you have to ask God to make up the difference. You will run low for many days, but a good husband knows his source. He does not do it alone but asks God to lead him. Loving your wife is not an option; it is a command. For any commandment God gives, He is faithful and willing to help you fulfill it.

I will go out on a limb and say that if you are a husband, congratulations. You believe in a cause that is bigger than you. At some point, you looked at your life and made an informed decision. At least, I hoped that it was an informed decision. If not, I still applaud you and your efforts to live for a cause that benefits you and your community. If I may, I can go deeper. Your being married also benefits God as well. I know in all the excitement of getting married, we were only focused on ourselves and how great it was going to be for us to be married, but being a husband is what God and society need from you. God needs you to be a good husband because the Husband represents Jesus Christ and his relationship with his bride, the church. So when society sees you, they should see a duplicate of how Jesus treats the church. Okay, take some deep breaths. You are halfway there. The most significant decision was to get married. So often, it is easier to date than to get married. If you are dating, you can leave, but it is a deeper commitment when you are married. I'm sure you have heard," Why get married? It's just a piece of paper." I respond, " Well, if that is all it is, then it shouldn't be any problem for you to get it." The truth is that even if they don't know it in their heads, they know it in their hearts. Marriage and being a husband will always be a big deal because they represent one of the most incredible concepts of God. The family was designed to stand under this marriage umbrella and the Husband's umbrella. Removing the Husband eliminates the shelter that God intended for the wife and the children to stand under. It will cause the women and the children to be subjected to things that God never intended for them to be subjected to. The Husband was created to be a shelter; unfortunately, we sometimes need protection too. So, every Husband must know that God is his shelter.

When counseling women, one of their concerns is that they feel that the Husband does not have anyone visible to hold them accountable. The Husband would request the wife to follow them and often say," The Lord told them because they are the head." The woman would complain that they have to answer to a visible being in their Husband, but the Husband is only accountable to the unseen Christ. Despite being a false statement, I see the women's argument. In our defense, the woman can see their shelter and cover in a husband, but men have to rely on that same invisible shelter from storms, but I don't hear them complaining about that. I say that in the most lighthearted manner. Both Husband and wife have to trust God and function in the role God designed them for. Both need to count up the cost. Husbands need to make sure they can love their wives and the wife can receive the love the Husband is trying to give.

Husbands, the greatest advice I can offer is to make sure that whoever you decide to give your love to can hold what you are trying to give. It's nothing more frustrating than pouring water into a bucket with a hole in it. The faster you pour, the faster it will run out. We all have had issues that have left us damaged. You probably won't find anyone who hasn't been damaged, but you can find someone who has repaired the damage. The other challenge is to ensure you aren't trying to pour 32 oz into an 8oz bottle.

I love to see good husbands become all God has called them to be, but what is even better is seeing a wife who helps her husband become all God called him to be.

Chapter Eight

They Become What They See

**FATHERS PROVOKE NOT YOUR CHILDREN TO WRATH BUT BRING THEM UP IN THE NURTURE AND ADMONITION OF THE LORD.
EPHESIANS 6:4 KJV**

A father is one of the most incredible things you can be called in life. The title is more significant than doctor, lawyer, general, president, or CEO. Being called a father is an honor because it is also what God Almighty calls himself. That alone shows us the magnitude of the task and should be humbling to us. To be referred to as the same thing as God is a privilege and an honor. This sets a high standard for us who are fathers. Therefore, being a good father requires that you model yourself after the Heavenly Father. Even if you were raised without a biological father, you can always look to the one who can be a Father to us all. God is willing to father all who allow Him to do so. The trouble is that many of us want the provisions of the Father without following His instructions and discipline. We have somehow changed the image of what a father should be from what God has said into whatever fits our needs. We take advice on what it means to be a father from people who aren't even equipped to be a father. That's not to disqualify sound counsel, but it's always easier to tell someone what they should be than to be it. That's like me telling you how easy it is to be a pilot, and I've never even flown in a plane. I've seen a lot of movies with pilots, and my Daddy may have even been a pilot, but it doesn't qualify me to be a flight instructor.

So, what is the advice that the heavenly Father gives us? "Fathers, provoke not your children to wrath." This is something that we all must take heed. In today's times, we have seen fatherhood handled in many ways. Some use the "I'm the daddy approach... don't question my authority." Others use the "I'm your friend, and I'm fine with what you do because I don't want you to be mad at me" approach. The best practice is probably between the two. Somewhere that portrays that you are firm enough that your children know the red lines and that you mean business; meanwhile, you are compassionate enough to understand they will make mistakes. You allow them to correct their error. Admittedly, it is a tricky balancing act. You want to be firm enough that your children won't repeat their missteps but gentle enough that they won't feel like failures. This technique requires a lot of trial and error combined with a lot of prayers.

Proverbs 22:6 reads, "Train up a child in the way that he should go." Training is a process. Athletes train, and their training is not just completed overnight. They train day in and day out for years before they are ready to compete. When you become a father, you become a trainer and prepare your offspring to compete in the world. The trouble is that you can't train a child you don't spend time with. It is hard to train a child that you never see. Most children are not disciplined enough to train themselves. Too often, the training has either been cut short or never started. The value of a good trainer is priceless, but we have allowed others to disrupt our children's training while they still manage to train theirs. When a person, system, or principality shortens children's training, they have set them up to fail. If it is estimated that it takes 15 years of training to become an Olympic athlete, and we only train our prospect for seven or ten years, how would we expect them to compete, much less win? Of course, I can't tell you how long it takes to train a child because all children are different. I can tell you that the training is your job, and quitting is not an option. The training of our children has been cut short, and our communities suffer because of it.

Don't create the athlete if you are not prepared to be a trainer. If you didn't catch it, here it is again: If you are not ready to be a father, don't make the baby. Training a child poorly often is worse than not training them at all. How can that be? If a person teaches them incorrectly, they must be untrained and effectively retrained correctly. Sometimes, it's hard to unlearn what you have learned. It is often the poor training that provokes the children to wrath. Teaching children principles and concepts that don't work or constantly changing them provokes anger. Changing the rules or moving the finish line will encourage children to wrath. In other words, if you subject your children to the same treatment that many laws have subjected black people, you will provoke them to wrath. If you tell them this is the system and how it works, don't change it on them when they finally understand. If you and your child are playing a game and they are about to win, don't change the rules at the last minute. If you are playing basketball against your child and you two are playing the first to ten when he has nine, don't move it to the first twelve. Let them win if they can. You may never live it down if they win, but they will never forget it if you change the rules. Trust me, it is better to be the father who lost than the father who lied.

The text warns us not to provoke our children to wrath, but what does that mean? How do you provoke your children to wrath, and how can we avoid it? Provoking your children to wrath could occur in many ways. One way is by being cruel or unreasonably harsh toward them. You can provoke them to wrath by abusing them physically or mentally. 'To provoke to wrath' means to stir up anger in them. If you know something makes them angry, don't do it to make them angry or stir up wrath.

There was a time in the Black community when we believed a child's training was never completed. Regardless of a person's age, their parents still had the responsibility to train them. The parent could be ninety, and the child seventy, but the parent was still teaching, and the child was still obligated to be trained and was obedient! The training was a lifelong journey that did not end until death. This type of lifelong training added significant value and discipline to our culture because there was always someone you were accountable to and to whom you had to answer. Now, we've rushed the training process, and we push the children through because we have been made to forsake the responsibility of training our children. The system has made it so emotionally, physically, and financially exhausting that many fathers want it to be over.

Fathers must never forget what training was like and how to train. Remember what it was like to be young. A good trainer has first been trained himself, whether by another man or by God. Once he has acquired the training, he is to use that training to bring his children up in the nurture and admonition of the Lord.

If fathers teach their children how to play sports and not about God, then the father has failed. Even if they grow up to be successful and make millions of dollars, you have failed if you have not taught them about the Lord. You can teach them how to change oil, cut grass, and cook on the grill, but if you have not taught them how to pray, you have failed. Successful parenting is not measured by how much money your children make but by how many lives they changed. How have they treated people, and most of all, are they saved? Knowing how to call plays or rebuild a motor won't profit your child if they go to hell. The priority for a father should be to teach his children about God. Everything else is secondary! This text says that we are to bring them up in the nurturing and admonition of the Lord. Be mindful that we don't have the time that other cultures have. Our children are not guaranteed to make it to their twenties and thirties. Our children are hunted and stalked like prey, and you must teach them about God early in their lives. Statistics show that our children are taken away more often than those of other cultures, even though we are fewer in number. Whether they are taken by violence, drugs, or even the penal system, they are still taken, and once they are gone, so are the opportunities to train them. That's why it is imperative that we no longer take 'no' for an answer when it comes to training our children. We must stand defiant against anyone trying to take away our right and obligation to train our children. From when the child is born, you may have ten to twelve good years to complete your most effective training. If you miss that time, you will never get it back and will be trying to catch up from then on. Convince whomever you must to allow you to be a part of the training process for your children. It is your God-given right and your responsibility.

Chapter Nine

What's In The Name

> **Neither is there salvation in any other: for there is none other name under heaven given among men, whereby we must be saved. Acts 4:12 KJ**

What is the plan of God? Does he have a plan, and if so, where do you fit in? If you can't answer these questions about your life, you are probably frustrated by now. You may even be on the verge of giving up. While not trying or giving up seems easy, I know something easier. I learned something easier than quitting and throwing in the towel. Just ask him! Ask God what his plan and purpose are for your life. You may be saying," Well, that's not easy." Indeed, it's straightforward. All it takes is a little courage. If he answers, you are all the wiser; if he doesn't, you aren't less informed. It takes courage because God will hold you accountable once you ask and then when he reveals it. God won't hold you responsible for carrying out a plan he didn't make you aware of. He won't be angry about you not fulfilling a purpose he concealed or hid from you. That's not who God is. So, God plans to make his plans known to you. That's even if you don't ask. If you are running or hiding from his plan, don't think that by not asking, you can avoid it. You still will be held accountable. For mature people who want to know, asking is the easiest way to find out. Asking will be the easy part. Fulfilling his plan is where the challenges are. At this point in life, I'm sure you have tried things that were much harder than simply asking and didn't give up. Why would you give up on something so important? Where I would love to answer for him, I think you will believe it better if the answer comes from God himself. Nevertheless, if you have not asked or heard his answer yet, rest assured that he has a plan and a purpose and includes you.

The entire plan of God can be summed up in one word: salvation! Regarding salvation, there are two kinds of people: Some have it, and some need it.

Salvation means being safe, delivered, or rescued from danger, destruction, and peril. So God's plan and purpose for your life are, first and foremost, for you to be saved from harm or danger. One of the things that makes life so interesting is that many of us don't even realize we are in trouble. When have you known the lion to announce his presence to the antelope? He doesn't because the lion knows that the antelope would run away if he knew the lion was present. So even nature teaches us that the lion catches the antelope that isn't aware of the danger. The antelope are highly intelligent because no one has to tell them that the lion means him harm. They know to flee at first sight of the lion but they don't just escape. They also warn the others to run. God's plan is not just for you to be saved but for you to save as many others as possible. God doesn't just want you to flee, but he wants you to help others escape.

In the modern church, we speak on salvation as it pertains to when you die and the place where you will spend eternity. Although, salvation is much more than being saved from hell. Salvation, or to be saved, is also to be protected from things on the earth. Under the umbrella of salvation, there are more blessings than we generally think. Along with the salvation of God, we also receive the plan, the protection, and the provisions of God. These three things will not only ensure that you have a successful journey but also that you can have peace on your journey. God has given it to you, and it's up to you to ensure that nothing or no one steals it from you.

The scripture dispels the myth that there are many ways to go to heaven. While our journeys may all look very different, there is still only one way. It may seem bold or boastful to some to make such a declaration, seeing how so many other religions exist in the world, but I assure you that it is neither. I fully acknowledge a million ways to get to know God, but there is only one way to get to him. It is simply the truth in a world full of lies. Whether this truth will do you any good is up to you. You can embrace or reject it, but regardless, it remains the truth. If you embrace it, it doesn't make it more accurate. If you decline it, it doesn't make it any less valid. The truth is not contingent upon who believes it or not.

God said," Neither is their salvation in any other: for there is none other name under the heaven given among men whereby we must be saved." It is God's plan for you to be saved, and Jesus is how he made that salvation possible. Man's greatest need wasn't food, shelter, or clothing. His greatest need was for a savior. The only one that could do it did do it. Jesus the Christ, savior of the world.

The Protection of God

The second thing that every man needs from God is his protection. When we look at history, generations of men hold one thing in common. They all wanted to feel safe. Whether they built large walls around cities or if they bought large amounts of guns and ammunition, it's all to make them feel secure. Some had chariots and horses, and others had bombs and tanks, but all these products were designed to meet a need for safety. Safety for a man isn't limited to just physical. Guns and locks can protect you physically, but a man must also be emotionally and mentally protected. Black men are the most neglected class of humans on the face of the planet when it comes to being emotionally and mentally protected. There isn't a law on the books passed to protect the black man's mental or emotional health, yet tons of them have damaged him mentally and emotionally. A man's need to feel safe is vital to his emotional and mental health. Fear causes stress and anxiety that causes both psychological and physical harm. So, men have always been willing to go to great lengths to feel protected.

Even to his demise, he saves himself the best way he knows how from emotional, physical, and mental harm.

The need to feel safe makes the protection of God a key element in every man's life. I say with all certainty that whatever a man doesn't feel safe in, he will ultimately come out of. If he doesn't feel safe in his neighborhood, he is moving. He gets a divorce if he doesn't feel secure in his marriage. He will start a job search if he doesn't feel safe at his job. That tells you how strong and essential it is for a man to feel safe. Therefore, God has offered us protection to combat our constant need to feel protected. God always has and always will protect his children. By getting to know God, the protector, man can feel confident in pursuing God's will for his life. When you no longer have to focus on remaining safe from hurt and harm, it will give you the liberty to go after what is essential: God's will. The protection of God is the shelter that every man needs. Unfortunately, we have seen just about every class of citizen and even non-citizens protected, but not the Black man. Therefore, this overwhelming feeling among Black men is that we must protect ourselves.

We called, and no one answered. We cried, and no one cared. We changed, and no one noticed. We were submissive, and we were called weak. We were defiant, and we were called rebellious. We worked hard and were called lazy. We waited and were called impatient. We stood firm, and we were called stubborn. We arrived early, and we were told it wasn't time. We dreamed and were called crazy. I said all this to say if it seems like Black men have every excuse in the world, it is probably because they have heard every excuse in the world. When society can give you every reason in the world as to why you are not afforded the same protection and presumptions that others have, the protection of God is all you have. When your skin color makes you a perceived threat everywhere you go, even within your community, the protection of

God is vital to your peace of mind. It's hard to feel safe and protected when you are afraid to call the police for help because you are unsure if the officer who shows up will see you as the victim or the villain. This is far from what God intended when he created you. He never intended for you to worry or be anxious about anything. He wants you to be confident and secure in his ability not only to protect but to provide as well.

The following section in this book was written to introduce you to God the Protector. It will help you see that God must protect you, but you must stay out of harm's way. This means that you have to avoid not only the things that harm you physically but also the things that harm you mentally and spiritually. God is indeed a protector, but we have to do our part. Take the stress and burden off you and place it on God where it belongs. As you explore these eight principles, ensure that you are not making God work overtime to protect you from you.

Chapter Ten

You Have Help

When I cry unto thee, then shall mine enemies turn back, this I know, for God is for me. Psalms 56:9 KJV

God is for me! When was the last time someone reminded you that God was for you? When was the last time you reminded yourself that God is for you? You will not be taught that God is for you in school, on the job, or in most churches. Society is set up to teach you the very opposite. The shows on television, music on the radio, and even movies in theaters will depict that God is against you. How can God be for you with all the obstacles you face in the world and your home? It seems very unlikely, but it's true. The challenges you face aren't an accurate measurement of God being against you. Life has challenges built in.

God is for you! It may be your first time reading it, but I hope it will not be your last, even if you must tell it to yourself. Not only is God for you now, He was for you even when you were against Him. The Bible says that while we were yet sinners, God was for us.

If you are one of those people who look for signs or must have a signal to indicate that God is for you, allow me to say this. Don't! Don't look for signs of how well or how bad things are going as indications of whether or not God is for you. God can be for you, and things are not going well, but He also can be against you, although things are great. Too often, we have been told by society and even the church that adversity is a sign of being out of God's will, but that isn't always true. The devil is called the adversary, and that is because he is the one who *opposes* the things that we try to do for God. The devil is always the one that is against you.

Allow me to dispel the lie before I expose the truth. Just because you grew up in broken homes, experienced poverty, or faced crime-ridden neighborhoods doesn't mean God is against you. You may have prayed and asked God to help you better your life or situation without results. While the unfortunate things we face can be discouraging, these shouldn't be regarded as God not being there for us. Remember, the rain falls on the just as well as the unjust. Life's challenges will try to overtake us all, and during these times, we must remember that God *is* for us. He is still cheering us on and reminding us not to give up.

When life gets hard, and it seems like everything and everyone is against us, be assured that God isn't. First, He has no reason to be against you (not that we are without sin) further; I say that it doesn't profit him anything to be against you. He gains nothing by being opposed to you. The trouble is that we don't realize that God can be opposed to our lifestyle and not be opposed to us. He can be against the places we go and the things we do and still be for us. We have gone places, said things, and done some things He is opposed to, but He still is for us. God is perfect because He can hate our sins without hating the sinners. It may be easier to grasp the concept if you are a parent. Our children often say and do things that we oppose, yet we remain committed to them and their well-being. We are just as fully committed to their success as we were before they started to disobey. God is committed to our success even more so.

Consequently, when the enemy tries to tell you that God is against you, know it is a lie. It's just an attempt to keep you discouraged and to make you give up on God. Any voice telling you that God is against you will not be the voice of God, and it should be vetted. God will ask you why you are against Him, but He doesn't operate from a posture of being against you.

The man responsible for writing the scripture cited above was a man of God who had to deal with people constantly telling him that God wasn't for him. They would point to different issues in his life and his family as evidence. At some point, he determined that he would no longer listen to all the naysayers. When confronted by those who told him that God wasn't for him, he came up with the perfect response. He said," "When I cry unto thee (the Lord), then shall mine enemies turn back, this I know, for God is for me." David concluded that God was for him, not because anyone told him, but because of his experience with God. Your experiences with God will help you to see that God is also for you.

When David's enemies tried to kill him, he would simply cry to the Lord. Every time David would do this, the Lord would fight for and with David against those who would harm him. The Lord's willingness to fight on our behalf is also a privilege we can enjoy.

I began this chapter by saying that 'God is for you,' so you don't become frustrated with life and give up when times are hard. David didn't discover that God was for him by what he was taught but by what he had experienced. David said, "This I know." When you arrive at a point where you no longer wonder or doubt whether God is for you, you can have peace in all things.

As a Black man in America, you have every reason and right to think that God is against you. This has been programmed and replayed in our minds for centuries. Even in the church of old, they taught that our dark skin was a curse from God. Reasonably, it will take centuries to vacate this thinking. The good thing is that this message is from the outside and not from the inside. Using every type of media known to man, you can find some degrading statements about the Black man. The good news is that none of it starts from within. Yes, self-hate is real, but even those who hate themselves cannot say God feels the same.

It is troubling to consider why so much effort has been made to convince the Black man that God is not for him. Why spend millions of dollars to peddle a message that is not true? It is all about control. It's about an effort to remove God and replace him with human influence. Not just one human but an entire human race in an attempt to make one race dependent on another. The best way to do that is to remove anything or anyone seen as a valuable tool among the disadvantaged race. You create a system that depends upon the dire need of that disadvantaged group or race: to depend upon the other race for your medical, mental, physical, emotional, and financial well-being for its *existence*. Now, why would they tell you that God is for you and run the risk of you becoming dependent on God and independent of them? Even when you want to make a statement that your life matters, it turns into something so ignorant it has to be calculated. Why should it offend anyone for a person to declare that their life matters? It is only offensive to people who disagree. For me to declare that my life matters doesn't mean that I don't value anyone else's life. It simply means that my life matters, too. If my wife and I have a disagreement and I say that my feelings matter, she doesn't take it as if I'm saying that her feelings don't matter. She takes it that I'm saying she is being inconsiderate of my feelings. I've had cancer twice in life, and when I see people saying fight against breast cancer, I don't see that as an opportunity to say what about lymphoma? Lymphoma cancer matters, too. My point is that the statement Black lives Matter is only offensive in a society that disagrees. If I said save the whales, the only people who are offended are those who disagree. If I said save the trees, the only people upset are the ones who disagree. So the question is, why? Why would anyone be mad or upset about anyone trying to save anything or anyone from destruction? The answer is very simple. They are upset because they do not see the value in what you are trying to save. People will not help you save anything they do not value, including your marriage. So before we should ever ask anyone for help, we have to assess how much they value what is at stake. You don't have to beg people for their help to save the things that they truly value. This is how you can know who is really for you. You will encounter a lot of people in life who would have you believe they value black life but have no receipts. If you have to beg someone for help, they probably don't want to help you. That is why it is so insulting to God for us to beg him for anything. Nowhere in the bible will you find a place where God told anyone to beg him for anything. It is a misrepresentation of who he is. If we don't have to beg God, then why would you beg a man for anything? You have help and don't have to beg him to help you. You have to ask.

David didn't have to beg God for help when he cried to God. David cried out, and the Lord answered. Brothers, if you have not heard it, let me be the first to tell you. God is for you! I pray that your response is, "This I know!"

Chapter Eleven

Don't Hate The Harvest

BE NOT DECEIVED GOD IS NOT MOCKED: FOR WHATSOEVER A MAN SOWETH, THAT SHALL HE ALSO REAP. GALATIANS 6:7 KJV

Anytime the scripture begins with, "Be not deceived," it indicates that someone previously tried to deceive you. In this case, we are the culprits. We are good at deceiving and fooling ourselves when there is something that we want. We have become so comfortable deceiving others and ourselves that we also think we can deceive God. Not that it is possible to deceive God, but we try. Not because we are evil, neither is it out of disrespect, but often it is out of pain and ignorance.

We are trapped in the horrors of our past, and we conceal the pain and hurt because we think that God won't understand like other men have misunderstood. We have been trained from our youth to hide our shortcomings and weaknesses and conclude that there is no justice for people of color. Trial after trial, verdict after verdict, nothing seems to change. One generation after another, witnessing the devaluation and humiliation of men in front of their wives and children without consequence or redemption has caused irreparable damage. This societal standard has left many confused, and others enraged.

Meanwhile, those who aren't confused and dare to be conscious and 'woke' are marginalized only to be labeled as rebels and troublemakers. So, it would appear that there are only two choices. Either be angry or be asleep. The benefit of knowing God is that He is neither angry nor asleep. He has watched it all, and not a single event, no single injustice has gone unnoticed.

There is an attribute of God that many Black men have yet to see. Many doubt that it even exists. That attribute is of God's justice. Many have died hoping to realize it, but after living in a land of injustices and racial prejudice, those hopes have begun to fade with each passing generation. God will make things right, either on this or the other side. There has to be a distinction between our job and God's job.

One of the most remarkable attributes of God is that He knows real justice. He is the Attorney, the Judge, and the Jury, yet His verdicts are always accurate, and His witness never lies. Therein exists no corruption, payoffs, or plea bargains. He wasn't elected by men nor appointed by officials, so He owes no one any favors. God is the ultimate Judge of men and their deeds, and He will determine who is wicked and righteous. The comforting thing about God is that He knows everything about us and doesn't rely on anyone to tell Him. He doesn't have to check our references or background or spy on us through social media. He always knows the seeds we have sown in the light and the dark. He is not dependent upon man's opinion about man. He doesn't need our commentary to understand matters' depth or height. Neither does He need us to speak to the longevity or the lingering effects of it. He sums up His understanding in this simple text: "Be not deceived, God is not mocked, for whatsoever a man soweth, that shall he also reap."

This text says that God is not mocked. That means that He will always have the last word. That means no man will ever get the best of him, nor can they get over him. For whatsoever a man soweth, that shall he also reap. This text uses an earthly principle to teach us a spiritual truth. If you plant apple seeds in a field, you will be surrounded by an orchard full of apple trees one day. If you plant orange seeds, you can expect orange trees. So, what if you sow evil or corruption? What if you plant lies and deception? One day, you probably will wake up to a world you don't want to live in. Nevertheless, it is the world that you created. If you have things you don't want, ask yourself if you are the farmer planting all the bad seeds. If so, then stop it. Repent, and ask God for forgiveness. I've sown a bad seed or two in my life, but when I realized it, I asked for forgiveness and never saw much of the evil come my way.

Too often, we sow bad seeds and then blame it on the devil when the harvest comes. In reality, it was the seeds that we had planted and not Satan. I'm sure that Satan was there encouraging us to keep planting, but it was us who planted the seeds. The good news is that there is still time to replow the field and plant new seeds. It should also be comforting to know that those who have wronged and mistreated you will also have to deal with the seeds they have sewn. It may not come at your hands, but God will bring the same fruit the sower has sewn. I say this to comfort you because earthly courtrooms don't offer much comfort, but your hopes have to be higher than that. While the justice system here seems reserved for the rich and wealthy, God is still not mocked, especially not by the rich or wealthy.

Many times, we deceive ourselves more so than anyone else. God knows our deeds even when no one else does. We go out of our way to hide our deeds and motivations, but God knows our thoughts from afar. Not only does He know what we do, but He also knows why we do what we do. God knows our thoughts can be both comforting and concerning; comforting if your deeds are good and your intent, but scary if your motives for your deeds are impure.

We all have done the right thing for the wrong reason. We may be good citizens and morally correct, but God will judge that. God put a system in place to help us walk upright: sowing and reaping. Our lives are more than collections of fortunate and unfortunate events. Our lives are reflections of seeds that we have sowed and the harvests of that which they produce. Be not deceived; God is not mocked, and you are the farmer planting the orchard of your future. We can shift a lot of blame to society and culture, and in most cases, rightfully so. Yet, there also is a responsibility that falls on us. What have we planted? In many cases, we have planted good seeds, but the harvest is less than perfect. What do we do when we have done right by people and they seem to keep mistreating us? This is where knowing God, the protector, is vital. It's tempting to take matters into our own hands, but that is contrary to what God would have us to do. Jesus said, "Let the wheat and the tare grow together, and he will do the separating in the end." So, allow me to translate it into more modern terms. When a farmer would plant (sow) wheat, he would go out and plant good seeds, but when the harvest would spring up, weeds or tares, as the scripture calls them, would appear with the wheat. What do you do with the weeds that appear to be harming and hindering the wheat? Jesus said to do nothing but allow them to grow together. He goes on to say that because you don't want to harm the wheat trying to pluck out the weeds, We can learn from this that wheat is so valuable that God doesn't want anything to disrupt its growth. Sometimes, we do more harm trying to fix things ourselves than if we allowed them to grow together. We need to be mindful that wheat is a tall plant that grows from two to four feet tall, and at some point, the wheat will outgrow the weeds. It is at the point that the weeds are no longer relevant. I want to remind you that at some point, many things that have been bothering us and hindering us will no longer matter. God will raise you above the things that used to irritate you. He knows that they trouble you just because they can. He knows who hates you without cause, and we don't have to tell him who they are. He knows them all by name. At some point, all the things they have sown in your life will be the field in which they must live. All the lies, discrimination, segregation, and oppression that have been mailed out will one day be waiting in their mailbox addressed to them. Signed from God.

Don't hate the harvest. Just sow good seeds.

Chapter Twelve

Don't Use the Wrong Weapons

Recompense to no man evil for evil. Provide such things that are honest in the sight of all men. Romans 12:17 KJV

As a man of color, you will suffer more than your fair share of injustices. Most will not be because of anything you have done or failed to do. Many will come simply because of the color of your skin. In times like those, it is difficult to determine appropriate reactions. How do you handle people who speak negatively to you, follow you around a store, or pull you over for no apparent reason? Let's start with what your response shouldn't be to have a more productive dialogue.

Repay no man evil for evil. That does not mean that we have to ignore the wrong treatment or even tolerate it. We certainly are not obligated to pretend as though it didn't occur. It simply means that we are not to return to them the same evil they gave us. This is different from what comes naturally, but it is what is right. Yes, the Bible does say an 'eye for an eye and a tooth for a tooth,' but that would leave us all blind and eating soup. You can spend a lifetime trying to repay those who have wronged you and still not have repaid them all.

First, let me say that for most of us, our personalities prohibit us from returning that kind of evil. It is not even in our hearts or our minds. How do I know? History has proven it. After over 400 years of oppression, slavery, Jim Crow, and segregation, people of color have never sought to retaliate for what people have done to them. Think about it. Even when the opportunity presents itself, and we can repay some of the ills we have suffered, we don't. Why? Because it is not in us. History may try to portray you as uncivilized and uncompassionate, but these stereotypes are inaccurate.

Truth always prevails. What other race would permit foreigners to rape their women, sodomize their sons, sell their men into bondage, and not face retaliation? This wasn't because they were powerless but because it wasn't in their makeup. I don't say this as a bad thing or to depict cowardice, but to enlighten you about something of which to be proud. Even when some of the most tragic events in man's history have been inflicted upon us, we still rose above it all. Our long-suffering tolerance was not a sign of weakness but an indicator of true strength. Yes, there were riots and protests where properties were destroyed, but rarely a time of absolute disregard for human life. Therefore, listening to your heart and not your head makes it easier to avoid repaying evil for evil. No other race in this country can say they have suffered so much or as long as the Black race. The Christ in us has always prevailed, and I pray it always will. We have answered the call when the Bible tells us to forgive.

Considering that repaying anyone evil for evil is no longer an option, what other options are there? What can we do to deal with evil? You must know your limitations before you can begin taking on the task. You have to know that you can't change people, nor can you control them. You are ultimately only responsible for your actions. The challenge is not allowing your emotions to overtake you. We tend to make mistakes when we don't have time to ponder and consider everything. Think about how your decisions will not only affect you but also all of those that love you. Make sure that no one else will have to pay for your choices. Evil acts will not only cost you but also those who love you.

Further, when faced with evil, how should we respond? We might respond by portraying those things that are honest in the sight of all men. In plain terms, react in ways that bring honor and not shame to your name. You will ultimately be known for something. When your name is mentioned, it will provoke thoughts in people's minds, and they will be either good thoughts or thoughts of evil. For which do you want to be known? Do you want to be known for evil or good? To be known for good, you can't allow yourself to be overcome by evil. Do not be overcome by evil but with good (Romans 12:21). I'm sure you have heard of the saying fight' fire with fire,' but that is only if you are trying to destroy everything and everyone. To overcome fire, you must use water. To overcome heat, you must use cold. To overcome hate, you must use love. Similarly, to overcome evil, you use good.

It is a tall order to overcome evil, but it's possible. Doing honorable things is only sometimes popular, but it is always right. In our culture, it seems we are always on the short end of the stick, but that's because we forget who is measuring. The world counts who wins, but God measures who is right. I assure you that it will be better to be called the righteous than the winner on the last day. Don't get caught up in keeping score. It's easy to become distracted by trying to keep up with who wronged you and how you could repay them. Trust me, in most cases, it is not worth your time or your energy. By the time you repay them, someone will be looking to repay you, and the start of never-ending cycles could ensue. Sometimes, you have to rise above and accept the losses. Repaying someone for the evil they have done may feel good for the moment, but in the long run, it will keep you up at night.

The biggest reason why we can't repay evil for evil is because we are counting on God to bless us. We don't need to carry anything before God that is displeasing in His sight. We don't want to do anything that would hinder Him from blessing us in the way He desires. We want God to look at us and be proud that His children represented Him well. Allowing God to fight those battles and make things right lets Him know we trust and believe Him. It also shows our faith in him and not in ourselves. When we humbly give those burdens to God, He has to bless us for His Name's sake and, in the process, curse our enemies.

God has promised us protection, and there are too many scriptures to list to bear witness, but I love 2 Chronicles 20:17. It says, "Ye shall not need to fight in this battle: set yourselves, stand ye still, and see the salvation of the Lord with you." One of the most extraordinary things you can learn as a man is what battles are yours and which belong to God. I assure you that He does not need our help to win but desires your surrender. You have to allow Him to fight on your behalf. God will not enter into any battle unless you invite Him. Neither will He intervene because He sees you are losing. I know; you're thinking, "...you mean to tell me that God will sit by and allow me to get my butt whipped and do nothing?" That is precisely what I am saying. God isn't one of our boys who jump into every fight or beef that we may encounter. Although He has your back, we must remember that we instigated some of those fights and static! Some of those conflicts God told us to avoid. He told us not to entertain some of those wars; if we go in without him, He is not obligated to resolve them. So the next time someone wrongs you or directs evil toward you, I suggest asking God if this battle is His or yours. If He tells you it is yours, I assure you He won't ask you to fight it with evil. He will tell you to fight it with good and help you in your fight since you have sought His direction.

Providing honest things in the sight of all men sounds like an impossible task, but you would be surprised at how easy it can be. The thing about men is that we all have heroes from when we were young. We had characters that we loved to watch and cheer for. Some of them were fictitious, but we loved them all the same. The attraction to most of these men was that they were men who we deemed to be righteous. The hero would face some form of evil or obstacles that they had to figure out how to overcome. We loved to cheer for the good guy. We would even dress up and pretend to take on many of the same battles as our heroes. We understood that they were doing what they needed to do to save the day, and we were with them every step of the way. Well, it's no longer time to fantasize about being the hero. It's now time actually to be the hero. Without a cape or superpowers, saving the day is your turn. It's your turn to be the superhero in the story of life. It's time for you to set an example for other men to look at you and wish they had your courage, strength, and knowledge. Every hero needs a hero; you are just the right man for the job. When you provide things that are honest in the sight of all men, you become a hero not only of men but also of God. You demonstrate the very best that humanity has to offer. You can show all men what it means to be a disciple. Jesus stated," By this shall all men know that you are my disciples, that if you have love one to another," The demonstration of love is honest in the sight of all men regardless of race, creed, or religion. Don't use the wrong weapons. He has given you love, and God's love shall protect you.

Chapter Thirteen

Let It Go

BE YE ANGRY, AND SIN NOT: LET NOT THE SUN GO DOWN UPON YOUR WRATH.
EPHESIANS 4:26 KJV

One of the greatest lessons I have learned is that you can be angry about some things without being angry about everything. I was not naturally angry, but if I became angry, I was angry about everything. I didn't know how to channel or compartmentalize my anger. If I were angry about the job or school, I would also be angry about the car and the house. Even if nothing was wrong with the car or the house, the anger just took over. A better illustration is in how I dealt with others. If I was upset with someone about something, I was upset with them about everything. If my child brought home an 'F' on his report card, I would let that frustration transfer onto the basketball court when he played. I could not celebrate his success on the court because I was angry at his underachievement off the court.

If my wife spent too much money shopping, I would be angry and would not celebrate the home-cooked meal she had prepared because I was angry. I felt that if I had celebrated the good that people did while I was upset, they would think I was no longer upset. I was angry with them and needed them to know I was angry.

Many things in life will make you upset or angry. Many times, that anger is justified, but our responses are not. We have not learned nor been taught how to express anger in productive ways. Anger has been the justification for too many foolish acts. Either we can learn how to control our anger, or it will ultimately control us.

Fortunately, anger is a feeling and an emotion. Feelings and emotions can be controlled. Make sure your feelings only visit you and don't become permanent residents. Feelings and emotions change; do not make permanent decisions based on temporary situations. We have to live past the moment and see the bigger picture. If we invest the time to ask ourselves, "What would bring about the best results from our anger?" Many lives have been destroyed because we allowed anger to choose our destinations. Many have given up and walked away from hopes and dreams because someone made us angry. Ideas and relationships have also ended over someone's anger. We've abandoned gifts, talents, and purpose because we let someone or something anger us.

What if we didn't just become angry but also determined? What if, in addition to being angry, we also became focused? What if, in addition to being angry, we became steadfast? Anger by itself does absolutely nothing. So, put something positive with that temper and anger you feel. Don't let it be lonely. Balance your anger with something that will make your life better. Proverbs 14:29 admonishes us, as it reads: "Whoever is slow to anger has great understanding, but he who has a hasty temper exalts folly."

This scripture acknowledges that we will be angry, but we should not let that anger cause or lead us to sin. The Bible also warns, "Do not let the sun go down on your wrath." This text helps us understand that anger will have served its purpose at some point. Once anger has served its purpose and run its course, it is time to move forward. You have to know when it is no longer beneficial to be angry. When your anger starts to hinder your productivity or creativity, it may be time to let it go. The human body is not designed to carry anger for long periods. Long-term anger will produce things that are detrimental to your health and well-being. It could even shorten your life span. Lovingly, God has said, 'Do not let the sun go down on your wrath.' In plain terms, when the sun goes down every day, your anger should go down with it. If you notice, the sun doesn't just fall in the evening. The sun will gradually go down minute by minute and hour by hour until it is no longer visible. At day's end, your anger should go down minute by minute, hour by hour, until it is no longer visible.

God said, "Be angry, but sin not." If you aren't to the point where you can be angry without sinning, I suggest you don't become angry. It isn't realistic to be expected to live without becoming angry. I can't deny it will be challenging but worthwhile. Too many people are living a life of regret because they allow themselves to become angry and sin. They have broken laws and lost control, all due to anger. If you feel that you can't help but become angry, I suggest you find some effective counseling or behavioral classes to help you overcome it. In addition, it is always a good idea to get rid of the things or people in your life that make you angry. Nothing is mandating you have to keep people in your life that make you angry. It's better to distance yourself from things that make you angry than to keep them and cause you to sin.

Too often, we think that we can control our anger, but many of us can't. It is often too late when we realize that we can't control our anger. While the anger is often understandable, the consequences of uncontrolled anger are too dire to face. Unchecked anger will often move us outside of the protection of God. Think of it in these terms: the devil will use anger to lure you out of the safety of God.

Remember when that one sibling would hit you and then run and hide behind your mother or father? At that point, you became so upset that you would chase them in a rage and then end up in trouble.

You may have encountered a law enforcement officer who went out of their way to see if they could make you angry—stopping you for no reason and perhaps instructing you to lie down on the ground in your "good clothes" during the middle of the summer, knowing that the pavement is too hot for you to lie down. You are asked questions about where you are going... all the while delaying your trip. All these things are simply things the devil does to make you angry and provoke you to sin. Just remember that they want to irritate you and make you angry. It's all a trap.

I preach a sermon using a mousetrap. I brought out a mouse trap and would find a young person, maybe around school age, ideally between six and seven years old. I will ask them if they know what the trap is. They will answer, yes, they know what it is, and I will ask them, 'What is it?' They will reply," It's a trap." I then will ask them how they know it's a trap and who told them. They usually don't know who told them or how they know, but they know that it's a trap. I then allow them to take their seat and explain that they are correct; it is a trap. Not only was it a trap, but nobody present had to tell them it was a trap; they just somehow knew. The trap's design is straightforward and has not changed over the years. It has operated as an effective trap for as long as I can recall. Yet, if I set this trap and turn off the light and wait, it will catch a mouse in the trap if a mouse is around. I can remove the dead mouse, reset the trap, and catch another mouse with that same trap. I can do this all day until there are no more mice to catch. The amazing thing is that one mouse after another will meet their doom in the same trap. What is my point?

Generation after generation, we have been getting caught in the same trap. If your granddad got caught, your dad got caught, and your uncles and cousins got caught, why would you think you would not get caught? It's a trap. No matter what color you paint it, it's still a trap. You can spray perfume on it, and it's still a trap. You can decorate it all pretty and put lights on it, but it will still be a trap at the end of the day. You can't change the fact that it is a trap, but you can change how you approach it. You can make sure that you don't get caught. I'm presenting to you that anger is a trap. Please don't allow yourself to get caught in it." Be ye angry, but sin not."

Chapter Fourteen

You Asked For It

DEATH AND LIFE ARE IN THE POWER OF THE TONGUE, AND THEY THAT LOVE IT SHALL EAT THE FRUIT THEREOF PROVERBS 18:21 KJV

In the context of American history, the effects of unfamiliarity with scripture have had a devastating impact on Black men. These effects are still crippling us even to this day and have lasted for generations. The only thing more detrimental than the black man's actions is the Black man's words. Yes, some of our behavior is unproductive and destructive, but our words do far more harm than our actions could ever do. Our mouths have killed more people than our hands would ever kill. Our words leave scars that will never heal, burn bridges that can never be rebuilt, and dig graves that never can be filled. Our words toward and about one another have left trails of destruction that are only surpassed by slavery and Jim Crow laws. Our words have destroyed families, murdered dreams, assassinated characters, and imprisoned the innocent. Yet, our mouths are so dangerous that sometimes they corrupt their owners, turning destructive natures inward. This destruction manifests because we have forgotten a straightforward principle: Words have power.

Every word spoken either brings death or it brings life. Even more troubling is that not only do we allow people to speak death into our lives, but we also often participate. The words you have spoken and those you have listened to others speak about your life will ultimately determine where you end up. Imagine it this way: If you are lost, and you find yourself asking someone for directions, if that person gives you the wrong directions every time you ask, you will never reach your destination. That is what it is like when you allow people to speak negatively about your life. When they say that you are not going anywhere and will not meet your goals, they give you bad directions. They are leading you the wrong way, and you're willing to follow, although the directions slowly lead down paths you never intended.

We justify our words as well as the words of others based on facts and observations. Yet, the facts change with circumstances, and observations are subject to the one observing. In other words, facts are not final, and circumstances are not always the conclusions. You can't just know the facts; you must also know the truth. Something can be a fact, but it isn't necessarily true.

A good example is that in this country, white people believed Black people were less intelligent than White people. That Black people did not possess the same ability to learn and comprehend as White people. That is a fact. That is what they believed. History books and laws were written and passed to prove their beliefs. That was a fact, but just because it was a fact did not make it true.

So, how does this affect your life? You must make it your mission to know the facts and the truth. We live in a country that says that all men are created equal. That is a fact. That is indeed what it says. The truth is the laws and the system are not designed to treat all men equally, and they never have. Never confuse facts with the truth because the truth possesses a power that facts do not. The truth has the power to make you free, and the facts only have the power to make you knowledgeable. Knowledge is useless if what you know is untrue.

Every time you speak, you release potent words, and you must realize that. The words you release will either give things life or start to produce death. Your words may be honest and truthful, but what do they produce? Just because words are sincere doesn't mean they should be spoken. Even when you intend to speak life, you must make sure that you do indeed speak life. Your words will be judged by what they produce, not what was intended.

Let's look at three hundred years of slavery. Three hundred years of words being spoken and life and death being activated. Three hundred years of sentences, phrases, and paragraphs have been spoken and written. Words that didn't produce life. Words that didn't produce faith, hope, or love. Three hundred years of death, being spoken by greedy and oppressive slave masters. In conjunction with the enslavers, you also had the words of the enslaved people themselves. Slaves were not taught nor encouraged to speak anything but death. So, they learned the language and the dialogue that they were given. Even if their minds and hearts wanted to speak life, they were only permitted and encouraged to speak death.

One of the most significant revelations that you will have is what you say. The words you speak will not only give you direction but also provide you the means to get to where you are going. No, this isn't a 'name it and claim it' principle; it is a declaration of what you want, not what you see. If you are in a bad situation, declaring how bad it is does nothing to improve. It only makes it worse. You can accept the bad situation without making it worse with words. There's no need to declare that which clearly can already be seen. It would help if you said that which cannot be seen. That is why the enemy becomes angry when you change what you have been speaking about your situation. As long as you are negatively speaking death, then there's nothing for the enemy to do but watch you destroy whatever it is upon which you are speaking death. You are doing his job for him. The moment you start to speak life, he has to send haters in your life to speak death on that thing that you are trying to give life.

God has given us many examples of how we should and should not use our words. First, he makes us aware that the tongue can hold the power of life and death- not life alone, but death and life. That means that on any given day, at any given time, you have the power to change your situation for the better or the worse.

Consider your words like a dog whistle. If you blow a dog whistle and keep blowing it, and dogs emerge in response, whose fault is it? If you don't want dogs in your life, then stop blowing the whistle. If you have a duck call, blow the duck call, and ducks emerge, then who can you blame? My point is that if there is anything that you don't want in your life, then stop calling it. If you stop calling it, it will stop showing up. God Himself does not even show up in your life until you call him. He said, "Call Me while I am yet near and seek Me while I may be found,' If you confess with your mouth and believe in your heart." The confession is your speaking life.

God wants us to be careful with our words, not only about our lives but also about the lives of others. God doesn't want us to say anything about anyone that we wouldn't want to be said about us. He tells us that when we speak, it produces fruit. You will ultimately have to eat a fruit that produces either life or death, regardless of which you produce.

Proverbs 13:3 says," He that keepeth his mouth keepeth his life." God wants to protect you, but if you keep undoing what He is trying to do with your words, whose fault is it? It is hard to protect someone who keeps running out into traffic, and that is, in essence, what many of us do with our words by comparison. We put ourselves in harm's way with the things that we say. We not only do it to ourselves but also inflict this harm on our friends, family, and co-workers. We speak death over our cars, jobs, and finances and ask God why our lives are less than He promised. As a rule of thumb, you should never say anything God has not said about your life. If God has said it about your life, you can declare what He has already spoken. If He says you are rich, you should say what He said. If He said you are blessed, you should say what He said. He said that you are the head and not the tail, and you shall lend but not borrow. That is what God has said, and if you are saying anything to the contrary, you are wrong. God is looking at many of us while shaking His head, wondering why we won't say what He said.

Change in your life doesn't start with better jobs or education; it starts with better vocabulary. Change begins by saying better words and thinking better thoughts. It starts by turning off the death cycles and turning on life cycles by declaring what God has said and agreeing with Him.

Chapter Fifteen

Did I Hear You Right

BE NOT DECEIVED: EVIL COMMUNICATIONS CORRUPT GOOD MANNERS. I CORINTHIANS 15:33, KJV

This scripture starts us off with the reminder that the possibility of being deceived is real. It is a warning for all who are willing to heed it. The warning is simple. The company you keep will play a role in your success or your failure. While it may not be the people in your life physically holding you back, they may be holding you back spiritually or mentally.

Many of us have kept bad company for so long and have heard evil communications for so long we are now immune to it. While we may be immune to hearing it, we will never be immune from its effects. When I say that we have become immune, I'm speaking about desensitization to it. We no longer are offended, and hearing it no longer bothers us. When we were young, if someone said a bad word, we all would pause and chime in with a chorus of 'Oooh, whee!' That was because we all knew that something had been spoken that we all had been taught not to say. Now that we are adults, I don't expect us to react like that when something offensive or evil is said, but it should do *something* to us.

Growing up in a culture that views profanity as a strength and survival skill can be challenging. It makes it more difficult to escape. The rules were if you were verbally attacked, you had to respond. It was almost mandatory that you respond. Usually, the one that could be the most obscene or vulgar would be declared the winner. Usually, these exchanges would end without physical altercations, but that wasn't always the case. These situations often would escalate, not because of the two people in the exchange but because of bystanders. These people are more in violation of scripture than those in the exchange. When they promote violence and tension, their communication is more evil and corrupts more good manners than the two participants.

Evil communication is more than just bad or foul language. You can use words that are not considered profane, which is still malicious communication. All communication is not necessarily verbal. We are bombarded with evil television, movies, and social media communication. Many of the videos that are shared are evil and promote evil acts. Think of it like this: When a child falls or hurts himself and says a profane word, what makes him say it? He says it because someone else uses it in a similar situation. The child is just imitating what he has heard. So much of human behavior is learned behavior, so God tells us to be careful who we imitate. What we learn from others can corrupt the good things we have learned.

I know evil communication is sold as a sign of strength in our communities, but don't buy it. I hope everyone has a soft-spoken grandfather and grandmother, as I did. They demonstrated that power isn't measured in words but in deeds. They didn't resort to harsh words or profane language even if the situation warranted it. Instead, they used direct and firm words to convey the seriousness of their stance and commitment to their cause.

In today's society, this moral character is frowned upon by man but smiled upon by God. God has warned us that if you find yourself in a place where you can no longer recognize Him or yourself, it is probably an indication that evil communications have corrupted your good manners and left you in an identity crisis. No one can identify you with the God you say you serve when you no longer speak, act, or think like God. Be careful who you allow into your life. "Environment is Everything."

One of our most significant challenges is in our music. We love music and the way that it makes us feel. We feel empowered and energized with the right song ringing in our ears. Mainly because we tend to like music where we can feel the beat and lyrics. Unfortunately, the lyrics, in most cases, do not convey the kind of message or communication that God wants us to share. It is a difficult task to separate the lyrics from the culture. The music speaks to the struggles and often is written as an escape from a harsh reality called life. This isn't unique to black culture. Country music tells many of the same stories, just without the profanity. Being of the age when the music lyrics changed and they started to censor music, I'm very familiar with the evolution of hip hop. The industry of music publications went from condemning profane lyrics to promoting them. Our children can now access any song they like via the Internet. So now we have a generation in which curse words and profanity are part of their everyday dialogue. This is troubling for many reasons, but mostly because our young people don't know the power of words. They haven't been taught that "death and life are in the power of the tongue, and those who love it will eat its fruits." Proverbs 18:21. We have an entire generation that speaks death daily and wonders why it shows up. As a rule of thumb, don't call anything you do not wish to show up. It's the equivalent of having a neighbor with a mean dog, and you go outside and call the dog by name. You shouldn't be mad at the dog. He came because you called him.

We also need to be mindful of how we communicate with our children. How we communicate with them teaches them how to communicate with the world. If we curse and use profanity when addressing them, they will also curse and use profanity when addressing others. At some point in life, they may even graduate to the point of addressing you in the same manner. Parenting can be frustrating, but you should never curse your children. It does severe physiological damage that is hard to repair. Also, what if God cursed us? What if God used profanity (not that it is possible) when addressing you? You would never recover from it because every word would be accurate and indisputable. If God doesn't handle us like that, we shouldn't handle our children like that. Never underestimate the power that words have on a person.

Effective communication is a crucial life skill. I don't know an effective communicator that isn't successful. Being able to communicate and convey a message is often the difference between success and failure. That is, whether the message is good or evil. Communication is so vital that I can tell where you are in life and where you are going by how well you communicate. I can also listen to the people you surround yourself with and tell where you are going. God gives us a clear warning that evil communication isn't just a journey but also a destination. It's no secret when you arrive and wonder how you got there. You communicated every step of the way, and that is where you were headed. To no surprise, one day, you will arrive. Evil communication is always the mode of transportation to nowhere. The bus is full and crowded, but there's always room for one more. Make wise decisions because getting on the bus is easy, but getting off is hard. The driver will not stop or slow down to let you off. You have to make the same decision to get off the bus you made to get on. Just leap, and your good manners will remain intact regardless of where or how you land.

Chapter Sixteen

It's Available

My My people are destroyed for a lack of knowledge because thou hast rejected knowledge I will also reject thee. Hosea 4:6, KJV

As descendants of people denied the right to learn how to read and write, it is miraculous to see where we are today. After being sold, beaten, or even killed for simply desiring to obtain knowledge, it shows how powerful knowledge can be. People went to great lengths to get it, and others went to even further lengths to ensure we didn't. If some did manage to acquire it, there were still limits to the knowledge they permitted us to receive. Nevertheless, there was a rationale for their withholding knowledge. Society has always been ruled by those who were superior in knowledge. Anytime someone has more knowledge than you, they hold the potential to control and dictate your life. The thought of being controlled by someone you mistreated can be frightening. The Government took great care to ensure that retaliation would never occur. Laws were passed, and schools were segregated to ensure that one race would always have more knowledge than another. I can understand why. Can you imagine if the person that you mistreated all of their life suddenly had the only cure for your disease? What if the people you lied to and beat were the only ones who knew how to make bread, and you were hungry? Hopefully, these scenarios explain why the laws are written the way they are. It is so that the oppressed could never regain power from the oppressors. The laws are about power and ensuring that one group never obtains it.

People have always been held back or held captive by another group of people with superior knowledge. Whether they knew more about war, farming, or about God, those with more knowledge would rule and reign. In short, the people who held the knowledge held the future and freedom. The Africans were not enslaved because they chose to be enslaved. Slaves were slaves because someone knew more than what the slaves knew. The captors knew more about entrapment, kidnapping, and human trafficking. Due to the slaves' ignorance, the colonizers took them captive and enslaved them.

If a man builds a prison, the prison can only hold the prisoners, which the builder outsmarts. The jail can only confine the less knowledgeable people than the prison architect. The minute the prisoners become more knowledgeable than the man who built the prison, they will discover ways to escape, one by one, until the prison is empty.

An excellent example of this is when I had a dog. As a young man, I built a pen to corral the dog. Well, the dog escaped more times than I could count. He went under, over, and sometimes through the fence. The dog could only escape as often as he did because he was more knowledgeable than the man who built the pen. I eventually made a fence to contain the dog, but the dog taught me more about fence building than I wanted to learn. He could constantly escape because he was more determined to be free than I was to keep him bound. He certainly had nothing to lose and no consequences for his many escapes, so he did. Most of us no longer desire to be free; the rest are unaware that we are bound.

Black men and women have been held captive because those who have built fences have been smarter or more knowledgeable than us. They have spent years learning how to build fences, while we have spent years learning how to entertain ourselves while trapped inside the fences. We've spent years finding ways to entertain ourselves while in captivity, essentially to pass the time and minimize our captivity's severity. That's why they permitted our singing and dancing because as long as we were learning how to sing and dance, we were not focused on how to overcome the fences. The singing and dancing indicated a passive acceptance of the enslaved condition. The system does not want you to have the same educational opportunities because if you do, then fences will be eliminated by those with knowledge. If you ever come to know what they know, then they will no longer be able to hold you captive. Even worse, if you ever know what they know, you may also start to build fences.

What are the prisons and the fences that hold you captive? The best prisons and fences are the ones that the prisoners don't recognize as prisons and fences. Today's prisons and fences are not made of just walls, wires, and steel. Drugs, alcohol, education, and economics are what today's fences are made from. These fences keep us trapped in poor neighborhoods, schools, and communities. They have built fences, and you will remain trapped until you acquire more knowledge than those who made them.

Fences are erected for two primary reasons. Either to keep you out or to keep you in. The fences around the housing projects are to keep residents in. The fences around the suburbs are to keep non-residents out. Those are easy to recognize, but the economic fences are not easily recognized. Your financial status and finances are fences that keep you in substandard housing and out of the suburbs. They never have to worry about a flood of black people moving into the suburbs because of the economic fences that keep you out even when brick and mortar don't.

I don't think it's a coincidence that the projects have a heavy drug presence. Nor is it by chance that liquor stores are on every corner in some urban regions. These are the "fences" installed to keep you contained. If you happen to climb over the fence of drugs and sidestep the wall of alcohol, there are still these barriers: underperforming schools, violent neighborhoods, and racial profiling. All of these fences combined were constructed to keep you trapped and imprisoned. After constant exposure to these things, you'd begin to consider things normal that aren't normal.

So, God wrote this scripture to help us identify and conquer the fences in our lives. Hosea 4:6 says, "My people perish for lack of knowledge; because thou hast rejected knowledge, I will also reject thee. Notice what He said. My people are destroyed for a lack of knowledge, not money, education, or opportunity, but a lack of knowledge. Not for lack of food, water, or shelter, but a lack of knowledge is why the people perish. If you possess knowledge, you will never have to worry about lacking food or shelter because knowledge will help you obtain these things.

The only way to deal with the fences in your lives is by acquiring the knowledge of God. Someone will always be more intelligent, stronger, or wiser than you, but there will never be anyone smarter, stronger, or more intelligent than God. If you make it your mission not just to acquire knowledge but to practice and share the Knowledge of God, you will always be able to overcome the fences in which the world has tried to imprison you.

The scripture goes on to say that you have rejected knowledge. That means knowledge was available, but you didn't want it or choose it. It also means that you had the opportunity to obtain knowledge, but you failed to take advantage of it. Whether you were too busy, lazy, or prideful, each excuse leaves you in the same condition: trapped!

How did you reject knowledge? When was it presented to you? Knowledge is distributed free of charge throughout America every Sunday morning, every Wednesday night, and Saturday morning, if you like. It is shared in Sunday school, morning worship, and midweek Bible studies, and you reject knowledge whenever you do not attend. Every time you allow television sports or work to hinder you from getting the knowledge of God on how to overcome your fences, then God will allow you to stay there. He said, "Because thou hast rejected knowledge, I will also reject thee." In any fences you encounter, God will give you a ladder to go over, a shovel to go under, or the strength to go through. All you have to do is ask God for the knowledge He desires to give you. God wants us to overcome whatever is holding us captive, but without new knowledge, it will not be long before we are taken captive again by the new and improved fences.

Chapter Seventeen

You Are Protected

No weapon formed against thee shall prosper, and every tongue that shall rise up against thee in judgment thou shall condemn. Isaiah 54:17, KJV

Simply because you are alive, there will be some things that will discourage and try to hinder you. It's nothing personal, but there will be some things that we all will have to overcome. Take gravity, for instance. Gravity is something that we all encounter day in and day out. It pulls us down, and it slows us all down. Gravity holds us regardless of how big or small we are. Gravity doesn't hold one group of people down while letting others float around. When you are young, you can rise without assistance, but you may need help overcoming gravity when you are older. It's nothing personal. That is just the way things are.

Well, unfortunately, everything is not like gravity. Some things are personal. Some things are designed especially for you and people who look like you, think like you, and live like you. Some laws, policies, and procedures on restricting you have been well thought out. When you become aware that these things exist, life will become easier. When you know that society builds walls to confine you and hold you back, your chances are better to overcome them.

The Bible calls these impediments 'weapons'. The term weapons is used because it is clear to readers that weapons are used to attack and hinder the progress of the intended target. You were the target before you were even conceived. The same weapons designed to oppress and destroy you can ultimately end up helping you if you learn how the warfare is fought. The mental and spiritual weapons are often more dangerous than the physical. They even cause more casualties and deaths than physical weapons. Physical weapons are weak because they require an attacker to use them against you. They need operators willing to pull the trigger, swing the bat, or hurl the knife to work. Without a person willing to participate, the physical weapons are ineffective. So, if you live in a relatively safe community, chances are physical weapons will not harm you. Therefore, the enemy's weapons of choice then become mental and spiritual.

The mental and spiritual weapons are to discourage and degrade you. The mental purpose is to make you believe you are inferior, inadequate, and unbecoming. Self-hate is one of the most dangerous forms of hatred you could experience, and the enemy has been planting seeds of self-hate forever. If the enemy can make you hate yourself, that is less energy he has to spend because you will do all the work for him. He will sit back and watch you destroy yourself. Any time you start to exhibit behavior detrimental to your well-being, it is because someone has convinced you to form weapons against yourself. The enemy wants to destroy you, but he is counting on you to do it for him or to help him do it.

The enemy knows that if he can bombard a man with poor choices, he will likely choose one. Satan doesn't need you to select all of them, just one. He doesn't need you to choose drugs, alcohol, poor education, violence, and crime. He is OK with any one of these you choose because any one of them will serve his purposes. A neighborhood filled with drugs, alcohol, guns, and crime may eventually entice you. If a man doesn't smoke, drink, use drugs, or carry a weapon, he still might succumb while just being in the wrong place at the wrong time.

These are just a few of the weapons that are formed against you. The trouble is not so much in the weapons themselves as in not realizing they are weapons. Not seeing them for what they are. You will never win a battle you don't know you are fighting. You also need to know who is for you and against you. You must know who the real adversary is. It is more than just a man; it is a spirit. If it were just a man, the battle would have been over long ago when the man died. Because it is a spirit, it can live on even after men are dead and buried. Slavery didn't die when the Masters died. Segregation didn't die when men died, nor did Jim Crow or racism. These things live on because the spirit that prompted these conditions is passed down. So, if the oppressor's spirit lives on for generations, so does the spirit of those oppressed. Just as people are born with the spirit of a slave master, some people are born with the spirit of slaves as well. It's those very spirits that are the unseen weapons that are against you. All of those were weapons used by the enemy.

How can you win? Before winning, you must know your position in the battle. God has some instructions for you before you even begin to fight. God will put you in a position to win if you allow Him. Before He sends you to your station, He instructs you to change the battle plan. God said, "No weapon formed against thee shall prosper." This one scripture will shift the battle. Imagine going into war knowing that none of the enemy's weapons would prosper against you. I want you to be sober in your thinking. This text says that the weapons won't prosper, but it doesn't make you immune to some of their effects. It doesn't say they won't hurt or harm you, so you must still know their existence. Fighting an enemy whose weapons won't hurt or harm you is different from fighting an enemy that won't prosper. The word 'prosper' means succeed or flourish, so the scripture doesn't convey that the weapons won't hinder or slow you down. We sometimes waste too much time thinking about and worrying about things that will not affect us. The weapons of the enemies have distracted us from the essential things. If the weapons of the enemies won't prosper, then why fight? We don't fight because they can harm us; we fight because the weapons can harm others. I don't fight to save me; I fight to save others. It's about fighting for others until they come to salvation so they don't become war casualties. The weapons formed against me shall not prosper but will prosper against those not saved. Our mission is to protect those among us who will not or can not defend themselves.

When I was growing up, there was a cartoon character called Roadrunner. The Roadrunner had an enemy called the Coyote. The Coyote had all these plans and schemes for catching the Roadrunner. Nevertheless, no matter how elaborate or well-designed the plan, the weapons always failed. I can't explain why or how they failed, nor could the Roadrunner. I just know that they always failed. There are some lessons that the Roadrunner can teach us. First, the Roadrunner was never distracted by the Coyote. He just lived his life and went on about his business. Secondly, he never tried to stop or hinder Coyote's plans. He never thought he better get the Coyote before the Coyote got him—too many people who are supposed to be Roadrunners behaving like Coyotes in this cartoon. When you are a Roadrunner, you are too busy to worry about what the Coyote is doing because it will not prosper whatever it is.

We have dealt with the weapons the enemy forms against us, but what about the weapons formed against ourselves? Yes, there will be times when we will be our own worst enemies. The choices we make, as well as the paths we choose, can be weapons. We underestimate the impact of our decisions and then struggle to overcome the consequences. The enemy would have you believe that God is punishing you for disobedience, but often, we face not punishment but consequences. If a parent tells a child not to play in the street, and the child gets hurt, that is not the parent punishing the child. That is the child experiencing the consequences of disobedience. We have been led to believe that God does unloving things to discipline his children, while it is often not God but us. Even when we form weapons against ourselves, by God's grace, even those weapons fail. God doesn't say that no weapon formed against us by the enemy will prosper. He said no weapon formed against you shall prosper, no matter who created it, even if that was *you*. He said, 'Every tongue that shall rise against thee in judgment thou shall condemn.' Regardless of whose tongue it is, even if it is *yours*. God shall condemn it whether it is the President's or the Pope's. God is faithful to His word and is also true to you. If He said the weapons would not prosper, He had already seen and disarmed them.

God gave us this scripture so we would not be afraid to engage the enemy. So we would boldly go into the enemy's camp and set the captives free. When you no longer worry about the things that the enemy has planned, you will begin to do all that God has called you to do and become all that God has called you to be. So, now that you no longer have to worry about the weapons, what will you do? What hopes will you fulfill? What dreams will you go after, and what business will you start? Now that the weapons have been neutralized, what's next for you?

The Provision of God

The following chapters will only begin to scratch the surface of all the things and ways God can provide. God, the provider, is so much more than we can imagine. I think not only is it amazing how much he provides but how he provides as well. There are millions of millions of ways that God can bless you. He can provide money, counsel, protection, wisdom, faith, healing, and companionship, to name a few. To add perspective, he can do all of that before lunchtime. If you have a need, he has a supply. You will have the provisions to fulfill your purpose. If God gave you an assignment, he is obligated to provide you with what you need to complete it. He can't command me to forgive and not give me a forgiving heart. He can't command me to love and not give me the capacity to love. So, for everything God has called and created us to do, he has to provide us with what we need. God wants to introduce himself as the God who provides, but throughout history, things have hindered our view of God as the provider. Hopefully, these following chapters will help us see past those things that have impaired our vision. Yes, we were denied loans or charged higher interest rates than others. We were denied the right to buy property in specific neighborhoods. We were denied the right to attend certain schools and eat in certain restaurants, yet God is still a provider. Even to this day, there are places where you can't shop or play golf, but that doesn't make the word of God void. As you explore these following chapters, I was hoping you could focus on everything put in place to stop you. Think about all the mean and hateful things they do to hinder you and keep you from having what they have—going where they go and living how they live. Now, think about how none has worked. When you have that good fixed in your mind, focus on how God is faithful and doesn't need your enemy's permission to bless you. Think about how frustrating it must be to put all these things in place to destroy a people, and none of it works. Imagine spending day in and day out trying to find ways to oppress people with laws and statutes, and God keeps making a way. Think about stealing ideas and inventions, and then God gives them a better idea and a better invention than the one you stole. Think about how frustrating it must be to curse what God has blessed. Now, thank God that you don't have to be frustrated by trying to be Christian in public and hating your brother in private. Can you imagine how hard it is to wear a judge robe during the day and a Klan robe at night? How about wearing a preacher's robe on Sunday and the Klan robe on Monday? I say these things to show you that it's much harder to hate than it is to love. It takes way too much energy and effort to hold people down than lifting people. Think about it. If you and your sibling ever wrestled, it took everything you had to try to pin them down, but when it was over, helping them up was much easier than holding them down. So what's my point? When God is trying to reveal himself as a provider, it's much harder for people to block your blessing than for you to receive it. All you have to do is make sure that you stay in a posture and a position to receive what God is trying to provide. The following chapters will help you move into a position to receive. God is a provider, but you can't harbor hate in your heart and believe you can receive what he has for you. Now that you have learned how to accept his plan and protection, all you lack is his provision. The challenge is making sure you don't block your blessing.

Chapter Eighteen

Come On In

A MAN'S GIFT MAKES ROOM FOR HIM AND BRINGS HIM BEFORE GREAT MEN. PROVERBS 18:16 KJV

When you were born, your parents, neighbors, and loved ones declared that God had blessed your parents. While many were amazed at the new life God had allowed them to bring into the world, there was something equally impressive. In addition to the gift of life, there is another gift. It is a gift within a gift. God placed a gift inside the baby as if the baby itself wasn't enough. Now, we can celebrate the baby and the contribution that the baby will make to the world. Every child that is born comes here with a gift on the inside of it. That gift can be singing or painting. It can be writing or designing buildings. No matter what the gift may be, I assure you that it is there. God sent you here with a gift to do what no other person could. Yes, the world is full of gifted people, but your contributions are as unique as your fingerprints. We both may be doctors or lawyers, but our expression of our gifts will differ. We both may be construction workers or engineers, but our skills will still vary. Two men may be preachers, but their delivery styles will differ. Know that it's OK to be different. God designed us that way. He needs you to be you and no one else.

Living in a society that doesn't always value diversity will make you question your gifts. Are your paintings as good as others? Are your designs and ideas as good as others? Countless contributions of African Americans were rejected by society not because their gift wasn't good enough but because the culture wasn't ready to receive it from them. Sometimes, even worse than rejecting them, they would steal and claim their work as their own. History has shown us they may not accept you but are more willing to take your gift. They can deny you, but it's much harder to deny your gift. Society doesn't mind you entertaining them by running a football or dunking a basketball because that is your gift. They don't mind you singing, dancing and telling jokes. Yet, if you desire to own a business, buy a house, or become a politician, that may be an issue. I don't say that to discourage anyone from using their gifts. I say that so that you won't be discouraged and don't give up. You have to know that God will hold you accountable for the gifts he has given you, and he is not big on excuses. He gave you a gift not only to change your life but also the lives of others.

So how do you know that you have a gift? Matthew 25:14-29 tells a story about a man traveling to a faraway country. Before he left, he gave all of his servants talents. These talents were not the talents that you and I think of today; talents were a form of currency in the text. Yet this story serves our purpose perfectly.

To one, he gave five; to one, he gave two; and to the other, he gave one. First, you must know that he gave all of them something. They all had talent, whether it was five, two, or one. None of the servants could say that the Master hadn't given them something. The exciting thing is that he gave to all of them according to their ability. In other words, he gave them what they could handle. If he gave one five, it wasn't because he liked that servant more than the others. He gave him five because that was what he knew that servant could manage. When we were born, God gave us talents according to our ability to manage. He wouldn't give you more than you could manage. Therefore, we should never be jealous or envious of another man's gift because God determines who has what. What we do with what he gave us is totally up to us.

The story goes on to say that two of them used their talents to gain more, and one went and hid his talent out of fear. At first glance, this can seem like this is just a story, but it has many hidden truths. So many people today are hiding their talents out of fear. Many others don't value their talents enough to develop them, so they, too, waste their talent. Nevertheless, all of the servants had to give an account of what they had done with the talents which they had received. Those who had used their talents wisely were rewarded with more, and those who were afraid had the talents they had taken away. One of the most important things you can do is see your talent for the gift it is.

This text says that a man's gift will make room for him and bring him into the presence of great men. That means that your gift will be your mode of transportation. Your gift will take you places if you will allow it. Your gift was designed by God to bless you and to give your life meaning and value. If you are struggling in life, I ask you, what are you doing with your gift? If you can't make it, I suggest you pull out that gift you have been trying to bury and use it. Your way up and out of the hole is that very gift you have been planting. Your gift will open doors for you because you are gifted. Your gift will bring you favor and wealth. Think about it. Most of the wealthy people in the world are rich not because they were born into a wealthy family. They are wealthy because they serve the world with their gift.

One of the most incredible things about the gift that God has given you is that the world can't take it away. They can steal the by-product, but they can't steal the gift. Even on your job, they can fire you, but your gift walks out when you do. The devil works hard to discourage you, but your gift will make room for you. That means companies that weren't hiring will call because of your gift. That means businesses that have yet to open will ask you to come and be a part of them. When God says that your gift will make room, that means that if there wasn't any room or space, your gift is designed to make room. If you weren't on the docket and not on the program, get ready because your name is about to be added because of your gift. The only thing that you have to do is to be prepared. Be in a position where when opportunity knocks and it is looking for your gift, you can say," Come on in. I've been waiting for you and knew you were coming."

Chapter Nineteen

First Things First

> "But seek ye first the Kingdom of God and his righteousness and all these things shall be added unto you.
> Matthew 6:33, KJV

This scripture helps us solve one of life's most significant dilemmas: how to prioritize your life. How do you know what comes first or what has precedence? Setting priorities takes a lot of work with so many demands and obligations. We often need to be stretched more thin and overloaded with tasks. The scripture tackles this issue head-on.

'Seek ye first' tells us that the Kingdom is what we should pursue above all things. It says 'first' because we have been led to believe that other things have priority over the Kingdom. While it may not have been spoken, the world has demonstrated it. It becomes confusing when people put jobs, money, houses, cars, and even education over the Kingdom. We live in a society that values seeking everything except the Kingdom of God.

We can see the value of seeking cars because they provide transportation. We can see the value in seeking houses because we need shelter. We can see the value in seeking jobs because they provide income. So, I've concluded that we don't seek the Kingdom because we have yet to be taught the value of what it provides.

From our youth, we are taught to go to school and get an excellent education to obtain good jobs to earn a good living. I'm not devaluing these things, but there is another way.

First, let me challenge your thinking. Before we had a formal education system, what was the pathway to success? I'm referring to two thousand years ago when no school system existed. How did people live? How did they obtain clothes, houses, and transportation? Well, lifestyles then had very little to do with where they went to school, seeing how there were no schools as we know them today. They could obtain the things they needed, not by seeking things but by seeking God. They could have crops, herds, and houses based on their relationships with God. They would farm and fish to live and used prayer to ensure good harvests or catches. They knew that if they only needed rain to water their crops, God could make it rain. They knew if they needed a great catch, God knew where they needed to lower down their nets. Therefore, they understood that what they had obtained had little to do with them but everything to do with God. They knew that it started and ended with God for them to have the needed things. That's why it wasn't strange to them to hear Jesus say, 'Seek ye first the kingdom of God.' It is news to us, but it was only a reminder for them.

In our minds, we have become so self-sufficient and independent of God that He is more of an afterthought than a priority. Think of all the reasons that we miss church and Bible study. It's not that we don't have time; it's because we don't *make* time. There are still twenty-four hours a day, just as there were then. God played a crucial role in their decisions. Currently, we don't consult him until things are going awry. We waste time chasing things not worth catching, much less pursuing. The stress that comes from running after things that were already promised to us seems a little counterproductive.

God said He would supply our needs according to His riches in glory, not by how hard we work. Not by any means am I belittling work, but you should work for the Kingdom and not for substance.

Here is the problem when we work for substance. When we work for the substance, we say to God, "We don't believe You." "We don't believe that You will provide the things that You promised to provide." Yes, we should work, but our work is for the Kingdom and not just to make a living. When you work to make a living, all you will ever have is a living, but when you work for the Kingdom, you will have what you need in this life and the life to come.

When we were babies, where did we get food? Where did we get clothes and shoes? Did we work for it, or did our parents provide these things? Not only did they provide, but we also had the faith that they would provide. I have never seen a toddler on the unemployment line looking for work. They believe their parents will provide, which is all God wants from us.

In Mathew 6:31, 32, the two previous verses say, 'Take no thought for what you shall eat, what you shall drink, or what you shall wear.' Is this not the main reason most people will tell you they work? They will tell you that they are working so they will have something to eat, drink, and put on. They will tell you that they work to ensure that they will have these things. Yet, God shows his children another path. He shows us another way. He said, Seek ye first the Kingdom of God and his righteousness, and God will add all these things unto you.

This brings us to the harsh reality that many of us have been pursuing the wrong things for the wrong reasons. We can avoid some of life's frustration if we seek the Kingdom when we are young. Don't wait until you are an adult and have created financial obligations that you must meet. When you are a youth and still under your parent's care, seek the Kingdom. Ask God the plans and the purpose that he has for your life. That's when he can show you the job, the business, the career that he will use to provide for you to take care of you. Your education is a grand thing, but God never said it would supply all of your needs. That is God's job. God doesn't want us to waste our lives working for things he said he would give us. That's why so many people on their deathbeds regret that all they did in life was work for something and not for the Kingdom. When it is all said and done, things are temporary, and the Kingdom is forever. I've never seen or heard anyone on their deathbed say that they wish they had not wasted all their time working for the Kingdom, but I have heard many say they regret wasting all their time working for the world.

You need to ask yourself what you are seeking and why. Are you seeking it because it is what you want or because God has commanded it?

We live in a society that teaches you that there are all kinds of ways to get your needs met. Mind you, not all of them are right or legal. Yet some of them that may even be legal may not necessarily be right. With all of the options that are out there, there is one that is often overlooked. The most neglected way of getting your needs met is through God. This may be new to you, or it may even be your first time hearing it, but God wants to supply your needs. It is God's will, desire, hope, and ambition to take care of you. He desires to give you everything pertaining to life and godly living.

God not only wants to be responsible for you, but He will gladly do it. No one forces Him nor persuades Him to do it, but He does it because He loves you. Some people will help and bail you out, but will they do it joyfully? God will bail you out, and the best thing is He won't tell everyone that He did it. Sadly, many of us have not allowed God to supply our needs. We take on situations that God never wanted us to take on and then call on God to bail us out. I am not belittling that we call Him when we are in trouble because that is what we should do. As a good parent, nothing is more heartbreaking than finding out our children needed and didn't call on us. So it is with God. He wants us to call on Him, but He also wants us to take heed of His instructions so we can avoid some things as well.

In this scripture, God has taken ownership of supplying our needs. The most significant thing is that He does it according to His riches in glory. Not according to how good we are. Not according to how faithful we are. He does it because He is faithful and because He is good. By God's grace and mercy, we have the things we need. It is not even because we ask. After all, there are many things that He has given us even though we have failed to ask. There are things that I can't even think to ask, yet He provides.

The scripture says He does it according to His riches in glory. That means that we don't have to worry about layoffs or shortages. We don't have to be the first in line to meet our needs. He says he does it by His riches in glory because there is never a drought in heaven. There is never a layoff, draw-down, or cutback. If God supplied our needs according to earthly things, then His ability to provide would be subject to shortfalls. God's riches in glory will never run low or run out. You should prayerfully ask God to supply it when you have a need. He will often send it to you in many ways. It may be a job, a neighbor, a co-worker, or even an enemy. However, He sends it; ensure you are humble enough to receive it. It's God's job to supply, and it is your job to receive.

The last thing the scripture says is that He will supply it according to His riches in glory by Christ Jesus. This is the most critical part of this scripture because, without Jesus, none of it would even be possible. Think of it like this. All the blessings in heaven would remain trapped in heaven without the life of Jesus. Jesus became the route, the pathway, and the deliverer of all the benefits and promises of God. It is through him that we now have access to God and the blessings of God. Jesus opened a door for us that no man could open. Therefore, when we need a blessing, it is through Jesus that we should get it. For this to work, you must know more than just his name. You have to know who he is. I'm not saying you must be a Bible scholar or expert, but you must understand that he was more than just some guy who lived long ago. In truth, the more you know about him, the more access you will have to him and the Kingdom. The supply that God has granted us is unlimited access through Jesus Christ. If you have unlimited access to Jesus, you have unlimited access to the Kingdom. There's no need to compromise your character or morals to meet your needs. God never intended for us to take shortcuts to have what He promised to give. If we seek the Kingdom, we will have access to the supply which he promised.

Chapter Twenty

Give Him What You Have

But without faith it is impossible to please Him, for he that cometh to God must believe that He is, and that He is a rewarder of them that diligently seek Him. Hebrews 11:6

Is God pleased with you? Is He happy with how you live? If so, then how do you know? If He isn't, then how do you know? Can you measure if you are in good standing with God? Can you tell? Can you be sure one way or another? The simple answer is yes. You can tell if God is pleased with you. Yes, you can know where you stand with God; He wants you to know, too. Be careful because many people aren't sure about their standing, and they also want you to be unsure.

How can you tell if God is pleased with your life? First, let me dispel the lie. It's not by measuring all of what you may or may not have. The one sure way to determine if your life pleases God is by answering a straightforward question: Do you live by faith? If you live by faith, I can say that God is pleased with at least one aspect of your life. Where there may be other areas in which he is not delighted, God can be pleased with some areas while being disappointed in others. The places you walk in faith and exercise your faith in are pleasing, and the areas you walk in fear are unpleasing. The more areas you turn over to God and trust Him, the more areas will be pleasing to Him. When you evaluate your life, you may find that in some areas, you do well, while in others, you may need to improve. For example, you may be walking in faith regarding financing but walking in fear regarding your health. You may believe God to supply your needs and walk in faith regarding your food, clothing, and shelter, yet you are afraid to go to the doctor because of your family's medical history. Afraid to take treatment, afraid to take medicine, but at the same time, you are confident that He will keep your lights on. The irony is that the same God that provides is also the same God that heals.

The trouble is that many of us don't know God as well as we should. Nevertheless, God is always trying to reveal a deeper side of Himself to us, and the only way we can see it is through faith.

Faith is the road that leads us to God, but many of us are too afraid to travel it. We are so scared to travel because we aren't confident that God is at the end of it. If you knew, I mean, knew in your heart and not just in your head, you would boldly travel the road of faith. Yes, we have heard many things about God through friends, family, and church, but it's not about what you have heard but what you have experienced. The things we have experienced root us and ground us in faith. We appreciate what our parents and grandparents taught us about God, but that was their experience. We must have some experiences of our own.

Faith comes by hearing, but your life is changed once what you have heard manifests in demonstration and power. The only proof we have to offer that we have faith is when our lives match our beliefs. We all can say that we have faith and believe, but if there is no lifestyle to match our words, how can anyone know what you believe? If you live by faith, you don't have to tell anyone; they will see it.

This text eliminates much guesswork regarding how God wants us to deal with him. The Bible clearly says that it is impossible to please God without faith. That means we can offer anything else we like, but He is not pleased if we do not offer God faith. Think of it like this: everyone values something. The thing that is valuable to God is faith. You can pay a man who values money in cash, and he will be pleased. You can pay a man who values food with a meal, and he will be happy. You can pay a man who values homes with property, and he will be pleased. So, when we pay God in faith, He is pleased because it is what He values. Therefore, this should give us confidence in dealing with God because we know we are giving Him what He requires.

When you go to God, you have to go to Him in faith, believing He is who He says He is and can do what He said He will do. It's insulting to go to someone for help and openly doubt that they have the power to help. It's one thing not to know if God will, but another to know if He can. One is a measure of His ability, and the other is a measure of His will. We should never find ourselves in a situation that will cause us to doubt His ability because it's that ability that makes Him God. That is what distinguishes Him from anyone and everyone else. His ability to do the impossible and perform things only He can do makes Him God. It is like removing His identity if you doubt His ability (not that it's possible). How could you recognize Him aside from his ability?

Yes, His love would still give Him away, but even that is manifested through His ability to love when others can't.

Now that we know He can, how do we know He will? First, know that we do not seek God in vain. Every minute of the day we seek God is well spent. It is an investment with a guaranteed return. God said that He is a rewarder of those who diligently seek Him. That means that if you seek God, He will reward you for your effort. He didn't even say He is a rewarder of those who *find* Him. He said that He is a rewarder of those who diligently seek Him. That means all I have to do is stay consistent in my search for Him, and He will reward me. I would be doing you a disservice if I didn't tell you that you will indeed find Him if you seek Him. It's none that ever sought Him that didn't find Him. Nevertheless, He will reward you just for your effort. Keep in mind He is just as excited about you seeking Him as you are. You have something for Him as well. Your Faith! What does that faith get you? A reward! That is why the world will tell you, as a Black man, to seek everything but God. They will tell you to pursue education, jobs, clothes, money, cars, and women but never to seek the One who has all those things. Look at what is advertised to see what the world wants you to seek. I don't have to tell you to seek money, wealth, fame, or status verbally. All I have to do is flood your life with it, and you will naturally pursue it.

The matter concludes that when you have faith in God and diligently seek Him, you will discover that things will find you. On your journey in looking for God, you will find a job. While looking for God, you will find a house. When looking for God, you will find a car. God never intended for us to seek things. He intended for us to seek Him. When we seek Him, we have found all that we need. Never let your search be in vain. Seek God with a heart full of faith and a mind of determination. These things will not only lead you to God, but you will also enjoy the journey.

Chapter Twenty-One

Rain Or Shine

For he maketh his sun to rise on the evil and the good, and sendeth rain on the just and on the unjust. Matthew 5:45, KJV

Rains fall on the just and the unjust. This scripture should keep you from being discouraged. Stop waiting for life, to be fair. Life is many things, but fair isn't one of them. You can spend your days only keeping score, only to discover that the scorekeeper is the loser. Instead of enjoying life and playing to win, all they have accomplished is keeping up with the deeds of everyone else, never experiencing the joys of victory but also immune from the agonies of defeat.

It's easy to get caught up in admiring someone else's life that you can forget to enjoy yours. Wishing that you had all the chances and opportunities that others had will distract you from making the most of your opportunities. When you do that, you allow opportunities to pass you by. There will always be someone better off than you, but there is always someone worse off than you as well. It would be best if you never became overly obsessed by either.

If you take the time to think about it, is there much difference in men? It may be a difference in what they possess or own, but it's not a lot of difference in their struggles and challenges. Most of us have jobs, businesses, and families to provide for. Yet, we must remember whether our home is two hundred or twenty thousand square feet; they both serve the same purpose. They both are designed to provide shelter. If your car costs two thousand dollars or two hundred thousand, they both are designed to provide transportation. Both outfits serve the same purpose if your clothes are eighty or eight hundred dollars. They both were designed to cover you.

The enemy has perfected the art of making us believe a lie. The lie is that nobody has the same problems or issues as you. No one has the same obstacles that we have. That may be true. Problems are like custom clothes or shoes; they are often tailored and made just for you. Yes, yours may be slightly different, but we all have them. Some are larger than others, but the size of our problems doesn't matter. It's how we deal with it that matters.

Imagine two men walking down the street side by side. Suddenly, a storm comes, and it begins to rain. One man starts to run for cover while the other pulls out an umbrella and continues walking. What is the difference between the two men? Both men were on their way somewhere; they had to deal with and overcome the rain. Their solutions to the rain and how to handle the shower were different, but the men were still the same. The only difference between the men was that one man prepared for the rain, and the other just hoped it wouldn't.

So when God says the rain falls on the just and the unjust, it's not a comparison between the two men's character. Their character has nothing to do with it. If you saw the men, you could not tell the unjust from the just by appearance. Neither is the presence or absence of storms in a person's life an indication of anything. Storms only show the distinction between the prepared and the unprepared. It is a comparison of the two men's preparation. If the bible says the rain shall fall on both the just and the unjust, it indicates that you should be prepared and not surprised by the rain. Both men had the same opportunity to prepare. One took advantage, and the other didn't. This challenges and dispels a common myth that storms in your life are a reflection of your life. Storms do not indicate how good or bad a person may be. Storms are more of a reflection of seasons than of character. Regardless of how good a person may be, it does not give them immunity to storms. Irrespective of how bad a person may be, the sun will still shine on them. Yes, we can put ourselves in positions that bring about storms, or we can put ourselves in situations that bring sunshine. Yet, it is not us who chooses to make it rain or sunny in our lives. The part we control is how we respond to them both.

To live a fulfilled life, men must learn to make the most of the sunshine and the rain. God isn't interested in our ability to try to control either one, but he is interested in how we respond to them. A man who can't find a reason to be thankful for both does not deserve either. To become that in which he has called you to become, it is necessary to have both the sunshine and the rain.

Black culture has never taught us how to appreciate the rain because we feel like it's been raining our entire lives. We feel like our days in the sun are shorter than other men. There may be some truth to this feeling, but if God allows it to rain, he must also provide you with an umbrella. Sometimes, we have been so distracted by the rain that it never dawned on us that it has a higher purpose. It's a saying that says if it is raining, put buckets out. Putting out buckets is the best way to respond to the rain. We must put more effort into learning how to react to the rain instead of trying to prevent it. It has to be a shift in mindset. How do we take what God has allowed in our lives to benefit us? Imagine if you knew that there was a drought coming. Imagine how dramatically different life would be if you were smart enough to put out buckets, and after that, a drought arose. Suddenly, that which you saw as a liability would now be an asset in high demand. You would now be able to change your life and the lives of others. The moral is that no matter if your life is full of sunshine or rain, see it as a blessing and make the most of it.

Chapter Twenty-Two

Let Him Use You

And he said unto me, My grace is sufficient for thee; for my strength is made perfect in weakness. II Corinthians 12:9, KJV

In II Corinthians, God said unto Paul, 'My grace is sufficient for thee.' This scripture is hard to fathom when you spend your entire life in lack. When you have never had sufficient clothes, shoes, water, or food, it is hard to imagine what it is like to have sufficient anything. The word 'sufficient' is foreign to many of us. The word sufficient means to have enough, plenty, or ample. In other terms, it means to have no lack. If you lived in a society where everyone had the same amount of everything, then lack would be hard to measure. If you lived where no one owned shoes, it would be easy to be content because no one had shoes.

Nevertheless, we live in a society with an economic structure that dictates someone will always have more than you. Living life trying to obtain the most of everything will shorten our lives. Life shouldn't be measured by possessions or the number of things you can acquire. You may always be lacking in something, but one thing can help you deal with those feelings of inadequacy: God's grace.

God's grace is bestowed upon us to level the playing field. To make up for all the unjust and wicked things you may have suffered. God's grace is the ultimate compensation for the trials and tribulations of life. Grace is the unmerited and unearned favor of God. That means that you did absolutely nothing to deserve it. You weren't good enough, careful, or wise enough to get it. It's something that God gives you simply because He loves you. It's something He gives you not because of who you are but because of who He is. There are two things that you need to know about God's grace.

One is that it is free for you to receive. It comes with no cost and no charge. The second thing you need to know about God's grace is that it is sufficient. It is enough in all situations and circumstances. What does it mean to have an adequate amount of God's grace? It means that you have what you need when you need it. God's grace will give you a sufficient amount of everything when the time comes. If you need shelter, God's grace is sufficient. If you need clothes, God's grace is sufficient. If you need healing, God's grace is sufficient. God said he would supply our needs according to His riches in glory through Christ Jesus. God's strength is made perfect in our weakness. That means that God's grace will make up the difference in whatever area we are weak or lacking.

What do you have in life with which you are satisfied? What do you own or possess that you feel like you have too much? What do you feel is better than you deserve and more than you ever could use? What do you have that you are amazed that it is yours, and it's mind-blowing that you even have it? Of what do you have, a surplus or an abundance? I'm not speaking of things that you don't want, but something that you value. How many did you decide? Five or six? Two or three? Okay, at least you named one, right? Surely, you have one thing in your life that feels like you don't deserve it, and it is too good for you. If you can't think of one, let me tell you why. It's not that you are ungrateful or selfish. It's not that you are spoiled or that well-off. You need help to name one thing you have a surplus of that you feel the need to share because you need to understand what surplus is.

Yes, I'm sure you know that surplus means 'extra,' but most homes don't have much extra. For the most part, our surplus wasn't anything you would want to share. You haven't been in a situation where you could afford to start giving things away. There is a difference between knowing what a surplus is and experiencing it. We've seen many other people and cultures living in abundance, but that's nothing that we have experienced first-hand.

The culture that we live in bombards us with advertisements from sunup to sundown. All of these are full of new products, items, and designs intended to do one thing: Create appetite. Create a desire for something you didn't even know you were hungry for until you saw the advertisement. Advertisers and marketing specialists are trying to spark cravings for things consumers are driven to feel they must have! If the item isn't featured on television, it's on social media, or one of your neighbors brings it to your attention and shows you something recently acquired. That's when we can justify purchasing something new and getting rid of some old things. Sometimes, we don't even get rid of the old ones; we keep them both and add them to our collections.

All of this is made possible by simply creating desires. It makes us view what we have in a different light. We never knew anything was wrong with that old phone, tablet, or car until we saw the new one. Otherwise, we were very much content with what we had.

Before I go on, let me pay tribute to our history. Since we have been in this country, we have watched other cultures obtain more than us. They wore shoes when we didn't have shoes; instead, we fashioned stiff leather strips and wood planks for our worn feet. They put on clothes when we didn't have clothes; instead, we used pieces of rope and twine as belts knotted around muslin sheets and flour and cotton sacks to shield our tired bodies from the blistering sun and cold. They had books when our books were tattered, leftovers, torn, ripped second-handed from schools that had intended to discard them. They even had food when we didn't have food. We survived on scraps, animal and plant segments, and remains that were refused from others' tables, stables, and fields.

I could go on and on, but I said all this to make a point. When you have spent your entire life watching others have while you go without, it affects you. When you observe others waste what you need, but they'd rather throw it out than see you with it, this changes you. It might cause you to start measuring things that you shouldn't. It could lead you to have a corrupt value system within yourself. It definitely might pollute your view on life. This tainted view of life will lead you to ask why they have it and you don't. Why do they live better than I live? Why do they have to come first and I second? Why do they get what is new, and I get what is left, handed down, or no longer wanted?

There's nothing wrong with asking these questions. They are entirely fair to ask and legitimate. The trouble is not the questions but the answers. If you answer these questions incorrectly, you may be led to live miserable lives.

First, you don't have less because you are Black as it pertains to God. Again, God didn't make you Black to punish or curse you. He didn't make you Black to become inferior or inadequate. God never said, *"I am going to make them less than other races or cultures."* God didn't, but men did. God never said, *"I am going to make them second-class citizens, ride at the back of the bus, or drink out of Colored water fountains."* God never said, "I will make them slaves or servants," but men did. So, the effects of what man has done are still present today. Just because you have less doesn't mean God thinks less *of* you. We wrongfully attribute the foolishness of men to the will of God. Mainly because men wanted you to believe that it *was* God's will and not their intention, that you should have less. They wanted you to think that their sins were the will of God. They wanted you to believe it was God's will for them to have and for you not to have. For them to rule and reign over you and for you to be servants. The truth is that God is not a respecter of persons. That means He is fair and just, and it has nothing to do with your skin color. All men have grossly misrepresented God except for one. Jesus Christ! He never committed any hideous acts that we have seen perpetrated on humanity, nor did he condone any of them. Yet, for thousands of years, men and women who claim to represent Jesus have done things that in no form or fashion resemble nor reflect him.

Being treated this way has created hunger and thirst for things more so than a hunger for God. Our pursuit of equality has replaced our pursuit of God. We now chase things that are not even worth catching. We now desire possessions more than we do righteousness. In many cities, overcoming poverty and day-to-day living has become the ultimate goal. Admittedly, it is hard to seek God when you are hungry. It's hard to seek God when you are cold and need shelter. Also, watching those with food and shelter who do not even serve God leaves one confused. So, let's bring some clarity.

Everyone on earth should know what it feels like to have the best of something, even if it is just for a week or a day. We all should experience what it feels like to have the best car, home, shoes, clothes, or food. It doesn't matter what it is, but you should experience it at least once. Having the best of something will help you overcome your obsession with things. When you have never had the best of anything, it puts you on a never-ending pursuit of things. Have you ever seen people who have never had anything when they finally get something? They feel a sense of pride and accomplishment. They hold their heads up high and no longer feel that weight of always being second best and never first. Everyone should know what it feels like to win. Winning will evoke a sense of victory and value that losing could never do.

Anyone can lose, but it is more important that you learn how to win. Just because you fail doesn't make you a loser; it simply means you didn't win. Don't allow others to define your victories and defeats. Many people have won and don't even know it. The main reason is that we have allowed the devil to keep moving the finish line. If you run a race without a finish line, how do you know if you've won or when the race has ended? The movement of the finish line is designed to frustrate and discourage you. Not having clear goals for yourself can lead to depression and low self-esteem. You must learn to set personal goals and celebrate yourself when you reach them. You will never be happy with anything else, including God, until you learn to be satisfied with yourself.

Despite how much or how little you have obtained in this world, know that there is one thing you can possess that will always be sufficient: God's grace.

Chapter Twenty-Three

He Has Something For You

Fear not, little flock; for it is your Father's good pleasure to give you the kingdom. Luke 12:32 KJV

We often see God through the lens in which we see our parents. After all, it was their job to do everything we count on God to do. Then we came to realize it was God providing through our parents. Therefore, our parents play a huge role in our perceptions of God. If you have good parents, believing that God is good is easier. If you have bad parents, thinking that God is terrible is easier. The reality is that God is good even if you feel that your parents were not. Even the best parents will misrepresent the goodness of God on their best day. Not to say our parents are not good, but to say how much better God is.

The trouble with most of us is that we will never appreciate how good God is because we don't see ourselves as being bad. We will never fully understand how good God is until we can wrap our minds around how bad we are. When we think we are good people, we tend to believe that, somehow, we deserve good things from the hand of God. When we allow the world to set the standards for good and evil, our measurement will always be off. God has always shown mercy towards those who serve him and those who do not. God is good to us not because we are good to him but because that is who he is.

Now that we understand God, it should be easier to understand who we are to him. We are his children, which does not change based on our behavior. He does not put us up for adoption because we misbehave or get out of line. He corrects us and disciplines us in love. Why? Because we are his prized possessions and his crowning glory. God, who created the heaven and the Earth, the hills and valleys, takes the most pride in you. You are who he shows off and brags about all the time. You are who he admires and adores and who he cheers for daily. You are the motivation for his wondrous acts.

Now that you know how valuable you are to God, you must also be valuable to yourself. You have to cherish you. You are your most valuable asset next to God himself. Stop protecting cars, houses, and bank accounts, and start protecting you. Stop investing in stocks and bonds and start investing in you. Invest in your mental, physical, and spiritual health. God's plan, protection, and provision are nothing without you. You are an essential piece to the puzzle. To help you to understand your worth, God and Satan are fighting over you. They aren't fighting over cars, houses, or land. Good and evil fight it out daily over you because they both understand your value. God is willing to allow us to lose things so that he may keep us. Anything that draws us away from him is subject to removal without notice. God protects us because we are so valuable to him. I know that it's things and people that we may hate to lose, but everything that you lose is not a loss. God has to remove items from us because we are more valuable than that thing or that person he had to remove. God will remove a job because you are more valuable than that job. He will remove a house because you are more valuable than the house. So, don't be anxious or afraid when God starts to remove things or people from your life. The text begins with encouragement and a reminder. It says. " Fear not." That means that regardless of what God has moved or removed from your life, know that he is making room for kingdom things.

Whenever you feel like you are losing things of value or significance in your life, remember that it's your Father's pleasure to give you the kingdom. Let's put that in perspective. What does" it is the Father's good pleasure to give you the kingdom" mean? What is it that God wants you to have? He wants you to have the kingdom. If you don't realize what's in the kingdom, that may seem like a minor deal to you. The kingdom that God wants to give you has more. More of what? Everything that you can ever need or desire. Think about this. The kingdom has more food, clothes, houses, land, joy, and peace than you can ever have on your own. Not only does it have more, but it has an endless supply of more. That means you never have to fear running low or running out. Remember that this wasn't your idea, even if you think you may run out. It was God's idea and his plan. God said that it is his good pleasure to give you the kingdom. That means that you don't have to beg or plead for it. All you have to do is receive it. He gives it to you and does it because it gives him pleasure. Giving his children the kingdom he has prepared for us gives him joy and happiness. Who are you to deny God's happiness? If it gives him pleasure to provide you with the kingdom, shouldn't it give you pleasure to receive it? You will never view a loss the same when you take on a kingdom mindset.

The kingdom mindset is that if a storm blows something away from you in your life, God can use the same wind to blow something to you to replace what you thought was a loss. When you know what the Father is trying to give you, you won't longer settle for less. You won't settle for a job when the kingdom has a business for you. You won't settle for a plan when the kingdom has a purpose. It's the Father's good pleasure to give you the kingdom, and you shouldn't settle for anything less.

One of the challenges is that we know a lot about church and religion but not enough about the kingdom. This is interesting, seeing how that is primarily what the bible is about. It's about a King and his Kingdom that is set up from everlasting to everlasting. That means this kingdom has no end. We are also instructed that if we seek the kingdom first, everything else will be added unto us. So, a good question would be, why do we not hear more about this beautiful kingdom that God is trying to get to us? It is mainly because we have it in our minds that we will create our kingdoms here on Earth. We will build our mini heavens and be kings with cars, houses, and luxury items. I have some bad news. Even if you do manage to build your little heaven on Earth, there is this thing called death that will come to visit you one day, and it will separate you from everything that you built, and your reign will end. The good news is that if you receive the kingdom God has prepared for you, you don't have to worry about that. To be a citizen in the kingdom of God provides not only for you in heaven but also for you on Earth. God has something for you, but it's up to you to decide if it is something you want.

Chapter Twenty-Four

What is a Blessing

THE BLESSING OF THE LORD MAKETH RICH AND HE ADDETH NO SORROW WITH IT.
PROVERBS 10:22 KJV

What makes a person rich? Money, houses, stocks, bonds, or even cars? Think of someone that you would consider to be rich. How much money does one have to have to be rich? A million dollars? Ten million dollars or even more? So what made a person rich before we had money? What made a person rich before we had cars or houses? God will change your mind about what you consider wealth and riches.

Many of us have grown up with a concept of what it means to be rich, but what does God consider true riches? If everything belongs to God, he knows what genuine wealth is. Are the people we believe to be rich wealthy, or is it just what we have been trained to think? I've found that the state of being rich varies from culture to culture.

If you ask a man living in New York City, he will have one definition of what rich is, while another man in China would tell you a different amount. Which one is right? They both can be correct, for being rich is a matter of perspective. Not only is it a matter of perspective, but it also depends on what you value.

Being rich is not just a matter of lack and abundance but also a matter of what is essential. If I take two men and place them in a desert, and I give one unlimited amount of money to the other, I give an unlimited amount of food and water, which one is rich? I assure you the one with the money would die a miserable death even with all his money. Wealth has to be measured differently from how we have been taught. If a man values family and has a large family, he would tell you he is rich. Even if he has a small family but values them, he will also tell you he is rich. Wealth is not just about quantity but also quality. If a man has nine cars, but none of them work, and another man has only one that does work, which is rich? It all depends on what you value. If you offer a man a Honda that he can drive every day whenever he wants and a Corvette that he can only drive once a month, which man is wealthy? Once again, it depends on what the man values.

So what if a man values God? What if the most important thing you own and possess is God? What if a man's heart desires and longs to walk closer to God? He does not need anything but wants God just because of who he is. Anyone who truly values God has reached an understanding of what is true wealth. When you arrive at a point where you no longer measure wealth by things but by your walk with God, you can clearly understand true riches. The scripture says that the Lord maketh rich, and with it, he adds no sorrow. The material things that a man has can be lost. You can lose your job, car, house, or money at any given moment, but if you still have God, you are still rich. You can lose nothing in this world that God can't replace. So, when the Lord maketh rich, it is not just about him giving you things, but about giving you himself. The wealth of man is in his possession of the Lord. The poor man is the man without the Lord. God's presence and absence in your life determines wealth and poverty.

Deuteronomy 8:18 says that the Lord gives thee the power to get wealth. It doesn't say that he gives you wealth, but he gives you the ability to get wealth. Anytime God gives you power, he also gives you purpose. He will never provide you with power without a purpose. You will find that people with power with no purpose will ultimately lose both due to abuse. So, the question is, if God gives you the ability to get wealth, what does he want you to do with the wealth? Does he want you to waste it on riotous living? Does he want you to waste it on parties and social events?

The logical answer is no, but what he does want you to do is to use the wealth. He wants you to use it to establish his covenant. In simpler terms, he wants you to use it to establish his presence on the earth and fulfill his promises. God is a responsible parent who will not give his children anything that will destroy them. What parent would give his child anything that would lead to their destruction? Neither would God. So, the wise thing to do is ask God what he would have you do with the power and wealth he has given you. Where does he want you to go, and where does he want you to distribute it? The most important thing about wealth is that God does not just want you to have it but also wants your sisters and brothers to have it. If you take the wealth that God has given you and use it to make others wealthy, God will bless you tremendously. You may feel you don't have anything that makes you rich, but I promise if you take what God has given you and share it with others, you will find God faithful to bless you with more. Keep in mind that wealth is so much more than just money. Wealth is whatever is valuable in the earth. Wealth is money, houses, cars, knowledge of God, wisdom, peace, and good health. God gives us the power to get these things, so the question becomes, what are you doing with the power he gave you? There are many things that God will provide you with, but there are also some things that he intends for us to work for.

Everything that you receive isn't necessarily from God. There are some things that the devil wants you to have, too. Jobs, houses, and cars don't come just from God but from the devil. The devil will send you things, hoping to pull you away from God. He will send items to distract you from God's plan and the purpose of God. Remember that the Lord maketh rich, and he addeth no sorrow with it. If the things you have been calling a blessing came with sorrow, it may not be from God. The second thing to remember is if it did come from God, if you use the thing he intended to bless you wrongfully, it will become a curse. The most significant difference between blessings and curses is how we use them. The Lord is very deliberate in who and how he blesses his children. He will not send you anything or anyone that draws you away from him. So many people have managed to obtain wealth in this world, but many days of sorrow come with it. Never measure your wealth or riches by a standard different from God's. If you have God, you have already obtained more wealth than you can ever work for. Let your work be to gain more God and not more things.

Never let money be your motivation. The allure of money has destroyed more men and families than anything. Money is a deceiver, and it has successfully deceived every generation of men. It has caused wars and the senseless destruction of nations and countries, all because some have it and others want it. Money can be a dangerous thing if it is in the wrong hands. The Bible says that the love of money is the root of all evil. I find it interesting that most people aren't so much in love with money, but they are in love with the image that money portrays. They are in love with the by-product that money produces. Because money is indeed seductive and intriguing, but it is not money that is evil. It is our relationship with money that is evil. It's perfectly fine to have money, but make sure that money doesn't have you. When I say that money should never be your motivation, I mean never. There is no situation in the world where money was the motive, and it ended well. Money is only a tool, and either you can use it, or it can use you. I'm not saying that money shouldn't play a role when making decisions or shouldn't be considered when trying to chart your course, but money should never be the deciding factor. You know what I will say if you have read the previous chapters. "Never trade your purpose for pay." Money is often what is used to get you to abandon your purpose in exchange for your pay. Have a relationship with money, but make sure it isn't a love affair, and be careful when dealing with people who have a love affair with money. If money is a person's motivation for doing something, when it runs out, they will often leave when the money goes. For some reason, we have become accustomed to saying that people with money are blessed, but that isn't what God says. We have to revert to what God defines as a blessing.

It is appropriate to love the blessings of the Lord, but It's even better to love the Lord. You will never find it anywhere that God has condemned the love of a blessing. Neither is the love of blessings the root of all evil. The challenge is in knowing what is a blessing and what is not. In Matthew chapter five, there is a list of things that Jesus called blessings. They included the poor in spirit, those who mourn, the meek, the merciful, and the peacemakers, to name a few. There are more, but notice what didn't make the list. It did not say the rich or the wealthy. This wasn't an oversite on behalf of God. He wanted us to know that those things do not make a man blessed. You can be both rich and wealthy and be living a miserable life. The true blessings come from the Lord, and with them, he addeth no sorrow.

Chapter Twenty-Five

Thank You Lord

He who finds a wife finds a good thing and obtains favor with the Lord.
Proverbs 18:22 KJV

The Black man's perception of marriage has been dramatically tarnished and, in some cases, even destroyed. The marriage covenant has been cheapened not just for Black Americans but for all Americans as a whole. The image and the light in which society portrays marriage are not very attractive or appealing. While these statements are sad yet true, have you ever asked why single life is characterized as glamorous and fulfilling and marriage as boring or confrontational? Why is marriage life portrayed to be a burden and not a blessing? The simple answer is to keep you from getting married. To keep you from seeing the power and the potential that being married can bring. It's one of those things where we highlight the bad and hide the good. We may think it should be easy to see the good.

Often, the good only sometimes manifests itself in the long run. In this automatic, instant society, anything that does not show us who it is and what it can do in the first five minutes will likely miss us. That is about all the time we are willing to wait before we lose interest or find something else to meet our needs. Collectively, these things come together not by accident but by design. Who is the designer? Well, who designed it isn't as important as being able to recognize it when you see it. If you can convince a race that marriage isn't essential, you then can persuade them that family isn't necessary. If you can convince them that family isn't important, then you can convince them that children aren't important. If you convince them that children aren't important, you can ultimately stop them from reproducing. Why does that matter? Anything that does not reproduce will eventually die off. This process will take a while, so to speed up the process, let's make the father despise the mother. Let's make the mother hate the children. Let's make the children despise each other, and because of all the animosity, God can't bless any of them the way he desires. God said, "Be fruitful and multiply," but your multiplication was designed to be a blessing, not a burden. So why would you even consider getting married when society turns what God intended to bless you into a burden? Even better, why would they do it? Why would society turn what God said was designed to bless you into a curse? When you can't make an honest living wage to support yourself, and the system says that your child's mother is entitled to half of the living wage that already wasn't enough, you can't help but be frustrated.

    God said to keep from being frustrated with life and its pitfalls. " He who finds a wife finds a good thing and obtains favor with the Lord." The first thing that we must know is what makes a wife a good thing. Is it her beauty, education, cooking, or how she manages a house? God didn't have those things in mind when he said it or created her. What makes a wife a good thing is when she is walking in the purpose and plan of God. God looked at the man and said in Genesis 2:18 that it is not good that man should be alone; I will make him a helpmeet. When a man finds a wife, he has found his helpmeet. It says a wife and not just a woman because every woman is not a wife and wasn't intended to be. Yet, if he has found a wife, he has found someone to help him fulfill his purpose. Every woman that you find will not necessarily be a good thing. Some will be good, but just not for you. Remember that just like God is trying to get some people to you, so is Satan. You may find many women but only one wife. Trust me, if you have found the right one, one will be all that you need.

Society has tried hard to make men no longer value a wife and marriage because it is all they can do to keep you from finding your good thing. If it can convince you that what you are looking for isn't worth finding, you will eventually stop looking. The world is trying to tell you things contrary to God's words. God said that if you have found a wife, you have found a good thing, but the world says she is not. Does this then become a question as to who you will believe? God blesses you daily with the gift of life or the world that makes promises and never delivers. God said your wife is good, and his favor comes with her. So, to keep her out of your life and the favor of God off your life, the world says let's confuse their mind and distort everything God has said about marriage. Let's distort everything that God said that a marriage can do. Let's distort everything that God has said that a marriage can be. If that wasn't good enough, the society said, let's distort even what God has said that marriage is.

The society said because there is a desire in a man's heart to get married and multiply, let's remove the desire. Let's make it unattractive that no man will even consider getting married. Let's make it so complicated that even if they get married, they won't stay. Society found that marriage was in a man's heart and not just in his head, and it was harder to remove than they thought. You can change what is in a man's head easier than you can what is in his heart. What is in his heart is not influenced by what you put in his head. You can teach a man to perform good or evil, but it will, at best, only be in his head. If you want to change someone, you must change what is in their heart, not just what's in their head. Information, at best, may change a man's mind, but God will have to change the heart. So, when they could not remove the desire from the man's heart to get married, they said, let's turn that desire from them wanting a woman to them wanting a man. By doing this, the man will be married, but he won't have a good thing in a wife, and neither will he have the favor of the Lord in his life. He will spend so much time in confusion and disarray because he will look for being married to a man to produce the things that only God said would come from a woman. He will desire to fulfill his purpose to reproduce and be fruitful, but the blessing can only come from a woman and not another man. He will look for a helpmeet to help him fulfill his purpose, but it will only come from a woman and not from a man. He will look for the favor of the Lord in his life because he knows it is supposed to be in his life, but sadly, it won't be there. It won't be there because the blessing isn't in getting married, but the blessing is in finding a wife. So, he knows in his heart that marriage is supposed to be more, but in his head, he thinks it's not because he has the wrong spouse. Yes, indeed, he does have the wrong spouse and the wrong kind of spouse when he is married to another man instead of a woman. All of this didn't fall into place by chance or accident. It was a planned distraction to keep men from being and becoming that which God has called and created them to be.

God said that he who finds a wife finds a good thing, and he finds the favor of the Lord. Notice that it says he who finds a wife, yet when you find her, she isn't married. She will not become a wife until you marry her, yet the bible refers to her as a wife. This is because when you find a wife, she will already do what a wife should do. That doesn't mean that she is perfect or complete, but it does mean that she already understands the basics. She should already understand the wife's role and is already working to perfect her wife's skills. She should already be naturally doing what will be required of her. Too often, men have married women perfect for dating, only to find that every good girlfriend does not translate into a wife.

When you feel it is time to seek a wife, please do not do it alone. Ask friends and family to assess your readiness to be a husband. Remember that you will make a young lady into a wife and become someone's husband. Sometimes, women cannot be good wives because men are unprepared to be husbands. We must be prepared to lead a wife and a household.

I will give you some advice that you should consider. If you are not ready to marry, you are unprepared to date. The whole purpose of dating should be to find a wife. You should refrain from dating if you are not looking for a wife. When you start to date someone, and if things are going well, the expectation is that you will marry. Many of us marry even though we are not ready to be husbands. We were only prepared to date but were trapped when the situation called for more than just dating. You weren't even looking for a wife or to get married, but that is where you ended up. Marriage is great for those who are prepared, but many of us are never prepared. We weren't looking for wives. We were looking for girlfriends, and the girlfriend standard often does not transfer to a wife.

God's plan is for you to be ready to be a husband, then you can date. Then, you will look through the proper lens and see that there are few that you would make your wife. You will be more selective of whom you will date when you know that dating should translate into an until death do you part.

When you are ready to be a husband, you can start looking to find that wife God has said is a good thing. He will lead you to her if you are indeed ready. Until then, you should keep developing the skills needed to be called a husband. God has and always will provide you with what you need when you need it, including a wife. God's provision covers it all, including a wife. God wouldn't withhold any good thing from you, including a wife.

Conclusion

So, what does the Bible say to the Black man? It says that you were made in the image of God and after his likeness, and we are called and commanded to live like it. God has provided us with purpose, protection, and provisions to ensure that nothing will tarnish the image that he has given us. Therefore, we have no excuses to misrepresent him in any matter. Yes, it is challenging to represent God on earth, especially if you think you can do it without him. It will transform our lives if we can find it within ourselves to ask him to help us walk, talk, and think as he does. What a powerful prayer! For those of us who have children, imagine if your children said," Dad, I want to walk, talk and think like you." "I want to be the spitting image of you." You then would give them purpose, protection, and provisions so they can represent you well. That is precisely what God has done for us. A Father's image is the most powerful gift a man or woman can give their children. I'm not speaking of just looking like him. I'm speaking about his character, authority, and his mindset. That is the actual image of him that our children need to see.

Our greatest challenge isn't food, clothing, jobs, or opportunities. Our greatest challenge is within our image and how we see ourselves. Image! It is a simple word with a powerful meaning. The image issue will plague every generation without a good mirror. Without a good mirror, you will think things are cute that aren't. Without a good mirror, you will think things look good on you that don't. Without a good mirror you say things and go places and do things that you shouldn't. This is not just a Black man's struggle, but all men have an image issue. Wrong image of self. Wrong image of each other and the wrong image of God. This wrong image comes from various places like TV, movies, social media, and even our neighborhoods. It becomes acceptable if we see the wrong images of ourselves long enough. If you see black people portrayed as slaves, servants, thieves, and robbers, it will then begin to challenge your self-image. You will buy into the idea that if everyone else conforms to those negative images, why shouldn't you? Who will be shocked or disappointed if you live up to the image that they portray of you? If you see people who look like you, dress like you, and speak like you, portraying a particular image, it will become your new reality. Before the movie Black Panther, when was the last time you saw a black superhero? We can always land a role as the villain because that is a more believable role for society to accept. A black superhero or role model doesn't sell because it makes parts of society uncomfortable even today. Your being successful and honest doesn't fit the image they have portrayed you. I think it gives even more reason to be a black superhero or role model because society doesn't want to see it. Even when we have men portraying the right image, society will not showcase them because of the power and influence that comes with it. We have been faced with generations of men and women who have image issues because they are getting their image of black men from the world and not from God.

What makes the image so crucial is that the word imagination comes from the word image. Imagination is how you see yourself and others in your mind. Your imagination can show you images of someone doing things they would never do. You can imagine people doing good, or you can imagine them doing evil. It is only an image, and most images are not real. When we use our imagination, it is either going to help us or hinder us. When we imagine the wrong images of God, it hinders our relationship with Him. When we imagine that he is something he is not, it leads to disappointment and mistrust. Often, it's not based on who he said he was but on who we imagined him to be. Having the wrong image of God leads us also to have the wrong image of ourselves. God said in Genesis 1:26 let us make man after our own image. If we don't know the image of God, then how can we know the image of ourselves? We have a habit of imagining things that are not true. We do this because of the images that we have seen. Let me prove it. What is your image of a husband? What is the image of a father? What is the image of a son? You will answer these questions based on the image you saw and were exposed to. That is, regardless if the image was good or bad.

We have to change the image and the imagination of men. We have to show them better images of God and of themselves. This is the key to becoming all God has said a man should be. It's just that simple. When you lay your clothes out at night for the next day, you imagine what they will look like when you put them on. If you get up and get dressed and they don't look like you imagined, you change clothes or make adjustments. This has to be the same approach for life. First, ensure you have a healthy image of God, yourself, and others. Second, imagine how you can improve those images. We will struggle in life until we deal with the troubled images we have seen and created. There is no way around it, and not addressing it is not an option. Knowing

God, the planner, protector, and provider, is the image men must see and duplicate. I hope this book changes how you see yourself and how you see God.

One of the hardest things about writing this book was deciding what scriptures and principles to use and what to omit. At one point, this could have been fifty scriptures that every Black man should know. Nevertheless, those we didn't include are no less important than those we did. The truth is that 9-year-old I needed something different from 39-year-old me. If I reach the age of 89, I will need something different. The reality is that the 9-year-old me and the 89-year-old me shouldn't both be portraying the same image. There is something wrong with me if I can still walk, talk, and dress like I did when I was nine at age 59. The Apostle Paul said it this way: "When I was a child, I spake as a child, I understood as a child, I thought as a child, but when I became a man, I put away childish things." The only way that is possible is if you use the mirror God has given us. Yet the word of God can speak to both the 9-year-old and the 89-year-old and make the principle relevant to their particular walks of life. If you asked any other man what scriptures they thought were most suitable to men, they might give you 25 different ones from the ones I gave. Some people may see that as negative, but I see it as a blessing. If someone else gives me 25 more scriptures and can teach me how to apply them to my life, I will gladly take those 25 and 25 more if I can. That is my humble way of saying everyone's experience with God matters. No person can fully understand and explain all scriptures; that was how God intended it. I need you, and you need me so that we both may be able to become all that God has created and called us to be. I pray you find hope and peace in this book and our shared scriptures and principles. Above all, I hope you will find 25 more that mean so much to you that you will share them with the world.

"When asked what I hoped this book would do"? The answer is simple. I hope this book is a solution to a problem. It will change how men see themselves and how they see God. I hope this book will teach black men how to manage their relationship with God and others. If I can teach men how to manage their relationship with God, that relationship will teach them how to manage all their other relationships. The relationship with God will instruct and counsel them on all the others. Effectively working on that one relationship will teach them how to manage them all. That includes relationships with wives, children, siblings, neighbors, co-workers, in-laws, bosses, contractors, and acquaintances. The relationship with God will help you manage relationships with people and your relationship with things. It will teach you how to manage your money, property, cars, houses, influence, investments, time, and talent. God's plan is for us to be good managers of everything he entrusts us. We can only do that by knowing God and what he said.

I'm going to leave you with this. John 3:16," For God so loved the world that he gave his only begotten Son that whosoever believeth in him shall not perish but shall have everlasting life." John 3:16 is fantastic because we can see all three aspects of God within it. It reveals the plan of God, the protection of God, and the provision of God all in one scripture. For God so loved the world is the plan of God. That he gave his only begotten Son is the provision of God. That whosoever believeth in him shall not perish; this is the protection of God. Shall have everlasting life reveal God's plan, provision, and protection. I wrote this book to help Black men understand God's will for their lives. It was to help them identify the things that are holding them back and things to propel them forward. Also, most notably, how do you distinguish the two apart? Many things are not necessarily evil, but that doesn't mean they aren't a hindrance.

The three personalities of God that every Black man should know are vital to his success. He should know God, the planner, to know his life has a purpose. He should know God, the protector, to feel safe and free from anxiety about life. He should know God, the provider, to know he has help in his time of need. By knowing these, a man can travel this dangerous path called life and reach his destination. Can a man travel without knowing these things about God? Absolutely! Will his journey be more challenging? Absolutely! A man can travel with or without a map. The man with the map can plan his trip. The man without the map may never know when he has arrived.

Romans 10:9," That if thou confess with thy mouth the Lord Jesus and shalt believe in thy heart that God hath raised him from the dead, thou shalt be saved." The greatest lie ever told is that God cannot or will not save you. You are a lost cause, and your actions are too bad for God to forgive. You have done too much, for too long, to be a candidate for forgiveness and salvation. God doesn't save us because we are good. God saves us because He is good. To appreciate how good God is, we must understand how bad we are (were). God says that while we were sinners, Christ died for our sins. He didn't wait until we stopped sinning; he saved us amid our sins. The only way that God does not save you is if you don't want to be saved. The truth is that there is nothing more important to God than to bless, save, and keep you. Above all, there is a process, and God is committed to redemption. Despite your skin's pigmentation color, God loves you, which must be enough for you. He never promised you that anyone else in this world would love you. He never said your mother, father, wife, or children would love you. For many men, that is our harsh reality, but there is comfort in knowing his love is enough.
Know that when life is hard, and it is easier to give up than it is to

press forward, know that you have a Father waiting for you at the finish line. He is cheering and applauding you every time you do the right thing. He is encouraging you and compelling you to keep going. Know that the trouble and trials of life are tailor-made for you, and they are custom-fit. The outfit that clothes us in trouble is the same outfit that God will use to reveal his glory. So, resist the urge to quickly pull off the thorns and the burdens we bear because of the color of our skin. We often see God's plan, protection, and provision through these things.

The Father is the plan of God. He planned and proposed your life.
The Son of God is God's protection. He protects us from the wrath of God by dying for our sins and interceding for us.
The Holy Spirit is the provision of God; he comforts and leads us into all truth.

Thanks so much for your support.
If you have questions about this book's content or need help applying it to your life, please email Trevor@williamford1899.us. For additional information, you may watch our YouTube channel, "Getting-to-Know-God."

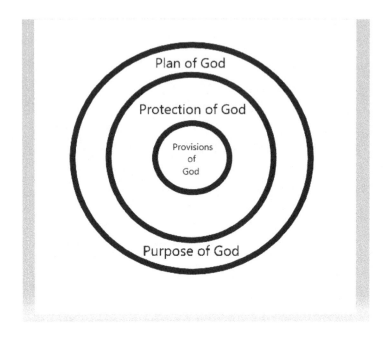

About the Author

Trevor is an Alabama native and a United States Army veteran who has dedicated his life to service. He is a licensed and ordained Baptist minister with over twenty years of service. He has spent years preaching and teaching God's word and motivational speaking. He also uses his gift for Christian counseling, life coaching, and mentorship programs. He has written several books but will tell you, "He doesn't write books; he writes solutions to problems." He has a strong passion for biblical truth and the life application of God's word. He believes application has been his foundation for overcoming life's most significant challenges.

He strongly advocates for peace and founded an organization called "Committed To Peace," whose mission is to promote peace everywhere for everyone. The organization aims to implement conflict resolution classes in the public school system. The ultimate goal is to have conflict resolution classes as a required curriculum for public school graduates. He believes conflict resolution is a life skill that everyone can benefit from.

Upcoming Titles

"'What the Bible Says to the Black Woman"
"What the Bible Says to the Black Couple"
"How to Do Business with God"
"Environment Is Everything"
"IF"
"Keys to The Kingdom"
"Thou shalt not be Black."
Go to www.WilliamFord.U.S or email Trevor@williamford.us
YouTube channel @Getting-to-know-God
Facebook William Ford Publishing